C000299168

Copyright © Philip T. Crawley
2014

Printed in Great Britain

ISBN 978-0-9564871-9-3

Published by Wyvern Media Ltd
United Kingdom

www.wyvernmedia.co.uk

The Game of the Sword

The lessons of Jules Jacob

Edited by Emile André

Followed by

The sabre duel and pistol duel

And advice for witnesses

Prefaces

by

Mr P. de Cassagnac, A. Ranc and A. de la Forge

Second Edition

Paris

1887

Translated from the French by P.T. Crawley

Acknowledgements

Very great thanks must be given to the following people without whom this book would not have been possible;

Kévin Côté

Kajte Crawley

Preface by Mr A. Ranc

I

The theory and method of the game of the épée that Jacob gives today in public are founded on his principals and on his certain experience that there are two modes of fencing: foil fencing and épée fencing; fencing of the salle and fencing for the duel.

Mr Émile André, in the introduction to this book, demonstrates, with justification, reasons which no one, who is not biased and is serious about the two games, can deny.

I witnessed the beginnings of this method in the little salle in the Faubourg Montmartre through which every journalist passed at the end of the Empire. I saw Jacob conceive the idea, determine and then refine the rules: I saw him work at perfecting them for two years. This is why I am authorised to write this short preface.

I also assisted with the first assaults where the new game was to prove itself. There was no lack during this era, even in Jacob's salle, of fencers who could not admit that duelling required special fencing. Of these, they were soon convinced of the fact by the touch of his button.

One day, one of Jacob's pupils, one of those who had worked at the épée method, entered an assault with one of his friends who always repeated that which is still heard again and again,

> "I will do in the duel with my épée as I do in the salle with my foil."

The two fencers were far from being of equal ability. The first knew his weapons well, but, due to being of poor physical stature, he remained weak even after long practice and had a somewhat mediocre performance. The other was a very fast fencer and who, at foil, easily beat his adversary six to three.

They went on guard. At the first engagement the foilist was disorientated by attacks to the arm, the leg, and the head. He

1

was not accustomed to protecting other parts of his body; he did not think to do this and was touched five or six times in a row, before he succeeded in landing a hit. He understood, and that same day became one of the partisans of the new method. Since then the proof was renewed twenty times in Jacob's salle and the result was always the same. Fencers who, in an all-in épée assault, affect to comport themselves as they do in a foil assault were invariably beaten.

Recall also, as I just mentioned, that some professors and also top-ranking amateurs support that one does in a duel as one does in the salle with foil in hand, that the same blows are possible and can be done in the same manner in both circumstances.

Alas, no, this is not the case!

These professors and amateurs will be defeated. They do not risk doing the same attacks in the duel as in the salle: firstly because sharps are used in the duel (a nuance for even the most resolute of men!); because they have a profound knowledge of fencing and extensive practice with weapons they will understand immediately that a change of performance is necessary.

Otherwise there will be a great chance that they will be injured by an adversary of far inferior ability or even be double-hit by a clumsy person.

You risk, for example, a quick disengagement and lunge. If you have an affair with an inexperienced fellow or, better, he retreats quickly and out of reach; or he lacks composure, having a tendency to attack in any line while firmly shutting his eyes. In these conditions there is never the certainty of avoiding being poked.

If, on the contrary, you have facing you someone practiced in the game of the épée, such that he retreats just enough to not be hit and launches at you at the precise moment that you are at the extent of your lunge and disordered. No matter what your ability your situation will be bad.

I admit, if you wish, that you will use your quick disengagement. If your adversary is not killed outright, which you cannot be sure of, while lunging fully and your épée contacting the body, retire fairly quickly to avoid a riposte.

And if you pass by him, if you miss the body, as often happens in the assault between those who regularly fence each other or even the best fencers, do you think he will let you- at full extension - return peacefully to guard? You will be happy if you do not pay for it with a nice épée hit.

It is enough, it seems to me, in this example to demonstrate the profound difference between the two fencings; I am careful when entering into a technical discussion to refer to Jacob's lessons.

II

Now, is the game of the épée, such as Jacob teaches, a new thing? Yes in that the theory and the professed method is, but not in the way that it has been applied in the duel. It is infinitely probable that renowned duellists of other eras had a special game, markedly different from conventional foil fencing. It is the case that two men that I knew twenty years ago, who had between them a number of fortunate duels, Mr Ambert, editor of the old *National,* witness for Carrel in his duel against Émile de Girardin, and Mr d'Alembert, who was personal secretary to Louis-Napoleon Bonaparte and one of the accused in the Boulogne conspiracy. One of Ambert's favourite sayings when he assisted in the assault was "Try to do this épée in hand!" and Mr d'Alembert said to me often "I thrust at the wrist and I riposte to the body". This is, in one phrase, the method of the duel.

I was born in a town where, during the Restoration and the first years of the rule of Louis-Philippe, many duels were fought. So often in my childhood have I heard the stories of the duels of this era. Oh! The duellists from Poitou who made their renown as dangerous adversaries, Bourbeau (a cousin of the old minister), Lemaire, the famed fellow from Pindray – to name a few - who were not the strongest fencers (in the salle). I got this from my old professor, father Nerriere, a master of the Lafaugère school, which Mr Legouvé may have known a little, and of which he repeated to me more than once that the Pindray, redoubtable, feared in the duel, worked seriously in the salle only after his most resounding duels. Is it not further indication that there are two fencings, the fencing of the foil, an admirable sport, but an exercise in convention, and the fencing of the épée, a method for combat?

I have just written the name of Lemaire, who some people will certainly remember as a peaceable Paris merchant. It is he that is credited with the words that the authors of "René Mauperin" put in the mouth of Villacourt, injured by one who had accused him of having stolen his name. Recall that the recitation of the duel which is one of the most beautiful pages of the book. Here is a true story where Mr de Goncourt had probably heard told to Mr de Villemessant who was related to Lemaire.

De Pindray and Lemaire fought each other at pistol. The adversaries walked up to each other, firing at will; De Pindray fired first. Lemaire, hit in the stomach, falls; but he rose back up on the spot and forced his finger into the wound, he said coldly to his witnesses the word of Villacourt, then he cried out to De Pindray who was leaving already; "Await my fire, sir!" De Pindray stood still and waited immobile. Lemaire fired and missed. My father who was a friend of Lemaire told me this anecdote a hundred times.

Returning to the épée; duels between masters-of-arms in this era were fairly frequent. The most noted was that of Lafaugère and de Bertrand, then de Bertrand and de Lozès. A curious thing, no one is certain of the result of the first of these encounters. According to Mr Legouvé, who claims to be an eyewitness, Bertrand had the advantage over him; his épée traversed the arm and chest of Lafaugère. Other faithful accounts from professors, well placed to be informed, say that, on the contrary, it was Bertrand who was injured. Lafaugère was not touched. Mr Legouvé must be the key to this contradiction. It is an interesting point in the history of fencing.

There is at least accord on the duel of de Lozès and de Bertrand. De Lozès received a slight épée hit to the shoulder and de Bertrand a nick to the base of the shin, at ankle-height. This proves two things: the first, that even in a serious encounter it is not as easy to kill as the Chamber readily believes; the second is that de Bertrand and de Lozès, two fencing masters, two famous professors, did not thrust, épée in hand, as they would in the salle; sharps sting.

And I finish with this aphorism of Jacob's "It is better to give a épée hit to the arm, then to receive one to the chest"

A Ranc

Preface-letter

by

Mr Paul de Cassagnac

My dear Jacob,

You requested a few line to put in your remarkable work "The game of the épée" as edited by Émile André.

Although I am one of your oldest pupils and hardly have the right to refuse you, I hesitate nevertheless, and with a natural modesty, to undergo this prestigious honour, if I shared it with two men who do not diminish its weight, Mr Anatole de la Forge and Mr Ranc.

As a trinity we can do what one dare not.

Twenty years ago, when we were but very young, and none of us at age of majority, I think, you were already a master, and I, much as today, a simple pupil. I loved weapons passionately and, free with my time, virgin in political matters, insufficiently held by the study of law in the Latin district, I willingly ran to the salle.

One day, I met at the home of Gatechair, near the Passage de l'Opera, a slight and elegant provost with no hair on his chin, just as mine was, who struck me quickly by his clear method and speed of hand.

It was you.

That same evening I spoke to my old professor, Grisier, who loved me tenderly and raised me with jealous care.

"You must take on this little provost" I said to him "in your hands he will become incomparable."

Grisier, the great Grisier, was cold, also a little stubborn and was not enthused easily.

He resisted. I insisted; showing him that his salle was insufficiently maintained, without a future as his teaching was without successor.

And you, having seen you in turn, he picked you.

You thus had the good fortune to enter the house of Grisier just in time to retain a professional and moral tradition.

He was a wonderful professor this old uncle Grisier, similar to those schools of masters which have now disappeared, who would not content himself to be only a hand or an arm but wanted above all to use his head.

Before long he could not fence any more.

But what a demonstrator!

He did not give a lesson, he reasoned as one reasons algebra or geometry.

And he did not allow you to do anything you had practiced until it had been grasped perfectly.

It had to be understood before fencing.

And if the opening sessions with him were slow, due to being fastidious because of their detail, perfection came about with astonishing rapidity.

> "Fencing" as he always said, "comprises not being touched, and then trying to touch."

I prefer this type of teaching to the sort of purely material, physical and almost bestial, where one breaks foils wrongly and crosses mechanically without understanding fully, for the most part, what one is doing!

Grisier, and those like him, never gave the same lesson to everyone, taking into consideration the differences in temperament and height.

He had one lesson for the tall, giving them the advantage of their height and holding an adversary at a distance; another for the short, teaching them a contrary art, to gain distance, and to stay there; he encouraged the weak to attack, the bold to be defensive, using these qualities until they became natural to his pupils.

How different, these days, are the masters who are above standard fencers and who imagine that they can communicate their speed-of-eye or quickness!

This is absolutely as if the great runners of the Pyrenees would wish you to learn how to make a journey of five hundred kilometres in only one day.

Also for me, the best masters are rarely among those who fence admirably, because they could not simply convey their natural talents; they are instead the ones who can make fencing a reasoned, powerful study and know how to adapt to each pupil the method which best suits them.

The little I know I got it from my old professor, dead today, named Fons, whom my comrades from Perpignan will recall, and who said about me with naïve pride, feeling good about his work:

> "He will go far, this lad, because he has an enormous lunge!"

Fons was one of the better students of Jean-Louis, the Jean-Louis before whom all men who worship at the cult of arms must bow religiously.

What joy it gave me to find, first from Grisier and then you, this classical school; simple, leaving nothing unexpected, enemy of all fantasy and which resolutely sacrificed the ambition of the touch of the button to the security of a parry, and to prudence in attitude.

Me, I had other things to do and I stayed humbly on this route, keeping from my masters, for whom I have no less love, who, with this solidity of principles joined with a solidity of heart, render a man sufficiently troublesome when épée in hand.

But you, my dear Jacob, you have achieved a great work, you have created the GAME FOF THE ÉPÉE, constituting the severity of this weapon, the sole truth of the particularly useless flourishes and occasional dangers of the foil.

One must, in effect, never, having gone out there on the duelling ground, confuse the épée and the foil and naively imagine that what one can do with one can attempt with the other.

Here is why good people, normally strong in the salle, find themselves completely disconcerted when they are faced with this relatively heavy weapon that does not bend, the épée!

I have had this disagreeable astonishment the one time that I fenced with a foil.

Instinctively, and as dictated by wisdom, I proceeded with multiple beats.

And, an unexpected result, if I pushed aside the blade it never achieved pushing aside the wrist. The blade would bend, ballooning, and I would get it straight to the face when it returned in line by it self each time that I wanted to launch myself forward.

Whereas when you push an épée aside generally one pushes the hand which holds it also and you can attempt to pass.

It is thus incontestable that, épée in the hand, on the duelling ground one cannot make a certain number of attacks.

It is this that is commonly called THE GAME OF DUELLING or THE GAME OF THE ÉPÉE.

It is this game which you have admirably condensed into a book, this game which you have made yours and which you embody for me and for others, one of the only professors capable of good preparation for the sobreness necessary for a duel.

In effect, the duel, today, and obligatory military service becomes a condition from which it becomes very difficult to escape.

It is imposed by the army, and everybody is a soldier at this time!

All heads of the family must thus henceforth place an épée in the hand of his son, not least that with this fore-thought the young man will become strong but so he will also be left in peace.

As fencing can be a hideous art, abominable, if you have the aim of seeking out quarrels.

It must be a protection contributing, on the contrary, to avoiding them.

And, on this subject, I cannot avoid laughing, while thinking on it, of those chaps in the world of fencing who have learned weapons so as to have the right to be eternal poltroons.

Their umbrella, their cane, their toothbrush is an épée.

Their washtub is mounted with foils, their razors possess a rapier guard and their chairs have pistol butts.

They all then talk about carnage when at home, and at the first quarrel, we all know such fellows...they flee like rabbits.

But I like better also those proud-at-arms of the fencing salle who fence, as ridiculous as they are, like those swordsmen of old.

And, I repeat, it is more honourable for the noble science of arms to be used to prevent an affair of honour than to use it to provoke one.

Yet, one must not give praise to these all too frequent encounters of our time where the adversaries have only one thought; bleed from a hand or arm and venture no further than the extremities of the human body.

It would be way better, reasonable to say, of adopting the method of German Schoolboys, who gird themselves with tanned hides and offer their adversary only those parts of the body which they have consented to expose.

The duel is grave matter and there is no excuse to conduct one except with this gravity.

It is no other matter, in effect, than a mean to remedy the insufficiency of the laws protecting honour.

In those countries where the custom and the legislation covers human dignity, the duel does not exist.

Amusing oneself by poking at entrails in this way makes the épée a lowly lancet, which may be hygienic but it is also grotesque.

Also we see witnesses inspired to find scientific and Latin words as a consequence to explain in a wilfully unintelligible manner whether he is touched on the back or the palm of the hand.

Many have sometimes criticised you on this matter, my dear Jacob, with great injustice, for having encouraged those blows which are shameful in the duel and the debasement of fencing.

Nothing could be more false.

And of those who do not know your lessons demonstrate the hand as the definitive target even though is it only a means of occupying the adversary in your way of thinking by threatening the nearest part, that is to say the advanced part, and which could easily be the knee or the head, depending upon the combatant's posture.

It is true that for a man who has never touched an épée you, or any teacher, have to give him a lesson which allows him to get by as best as possible and your responsibility will be terrible if you advise him of anything other than extreme prudence.

Also your lesson for the duelling ground, your GAME OF THE ÉPÉE is not to be shunned by an inexperienced fellow who has everything to learn and is surprised by an affair yet it especially also addresses those who already fence and who seek to improve their fencing.

It is said that the pupil, even if only a little, bears the celebrity of his master. But I do not hesitate to incur the wrath of critics of this sort and declare that you are to be considered a rare professor who teach useful fencing, practical fencing; that is to say the GAME OF THE ÉPÉE.

I speak from a position of disinterest; I have a wife and children, I am old and I am retired from affairs.

Nevertheless one should not, of those of you who doubt me greatly, accuse me of pacifist leanings and say that I am like an old warhorse who rattles his armour as he whinnies.

Also the joy I felt the other day was immense when I placed my little Paul, all of six and a half years old, on guard and I saw him instinctively make counter-quarte and then it amused me to deceive one of his simple parries. And I devote myself where possible to the management of the quarrels of others.

How many have I arranged? God alone knows!

It is a good deed and redeems my quarrels of old; and I often proffer every aid and every trial for those two persons who add their signature to mine at the start of this book in Mr Ranc, with whom I became a friend upon the duelling ground, and in Anatole de La Forge, a comrade of twenty years and honour personified. These two prove that the épée is not a bad object as it sometimes even brings together, with affection and courtesy, political gentlemen who have always been at odds.

You have asked of me, my dear Jacob, for only a few lines and here I am chattering away as we used to do in your salle between assaults.

You bring it upon yourself; it is a fault of yours.

Always with great affection,

PAUL DE CASSAGNAC

Preface-letter

from

Mr A. de la Forge

My dear Jacob,

You do me an honour by asking me for a preface for the book you are going to publish on "The game of the épée"

This pushes humility too far.

Ordinarily it is the masters who recommend their disciples, and not the disciples who recommend the masters.

What's more, is not your name alone the best and most useful of all recommendations?

A book on fencing, signed Jacob, is naturally called to encounter universal sympathy.

Those who know the concerns of the épée have the pleasure to learn new things with you, and those who are ignorant of such eagerly seize the opportunity for instruction with a professor of the *primo cartello.*

In your benevolence you didn't care, my dear Jacob, to embarrass me because thus one cannot speak of a book such as yours in a slight or mediocre fashion.

With you, one must begin (a preface is always at the start) with a masterstroke.

Your pupil, Ranc, is capable of these blows as is Paul de Cassagnac, another of your pupils, who is accustomed to them. These virtuosos of fencing are far more apt than I to sing great hymn of valour: they are envoys of their testimony to you; I can only add my best wishes.

I will add to them however a definition of your art, a definition that I think is superior. It is that of a man who became incomparable in the wrestling of the mind, one that understands everything and defines nearly everything. This genius, I do not flatter, would regard the science of fencing as the most liberal of all the arts "The science of arms" he said "consists of giving and not receiving."

Here is an irrefutable formula even on the duelling ground. And now we contributors, my dear Jacob, you, Ranc, Paul de Cassagnac and I would have not found better, even though we have the combined sprit of four!

But who was the author of this wondrous definition? Was it Roland one day when, tired from wielding Durandal, replaced with a pen what he was doing with a blade?

No, the author of this model formula was a bourgeois who did not love affairs, who mocked his captains and turned to ridiculing braggarts; but understood the requirements of a point of honour.

It was Molière!

Good French wits had graced him, for the loyal art of excellence, the definitive formula.

Molière was given the precept, your pupils followed the example.

I would not encourage, for sure, to abuse the advantages which you communicate. You make them strong, it is rather for their edification that they must not be quarrelsome. I will go further, and I affirm with your permission, my dear Jacob, that with your collaborator Mr Émile André that the more you possess the science of the épée the less one must be resilient to the arbitration of affairs of honour.

To fight when necessary- that is good.
To avoid a duel when it is honourable to do so- that is better.

But who decides between the rival protestations of

adversaries? The witnesses? They have too natural a tendency to identify with their client, they believe him exposed if they would not pull all of the blanket to their side.

Arbitration is thus necessary; but I must object that not everyone can be a judge and I agree that there must be some exception. The first of all, alas, is to not be too young.

If the first duellist of antiquity was Achilles I suppose that the first judge could have been Nestor? Homer represents him with a long white beard which must have suited him- particularly in the exercise of his duties.

I think that even the divine poet, to give him some solemnity in matters, made him swear during his fateful endeavours, "By Jupiter and my beard!"

Today Jupiter is discharged of his duties and the beard is no longer necessary. I call on this point the shadow of the judge, the clean-shaven and highly-recognised man of our times the Marquis du Hallay. He sports a fine upturned moustache, which hides nothing, or so he claims, of the épée of his adversaries.

Moderation of character is again very necessary in the duties of a judge, more so than the weight of his years; if only every time, in the matters of an affair of honour, there was recourse to the intervention of men of cold blood and heart, as these things that will bring a peaceful end.

It is thus with reason that our friend, the regretful Marquis du Hallay, could say,

> "I spent half my life in combat and the second half arranging the affairs of others"

The example that this incomparable judge had given is followed today by the Press of every opinion and in the parliamentary world. In the Chambers, both the right and left, all relinquish to the authority of the President for a definitive decision. In the Senate, due to a difference in temperament, they prepare laws against the duel.

The best of these laws, my dear Jacob, is your excellent and classic teaching.

We do not seek out affairs when one knows that they are serious and those of which you who have been taught how to use an épée have not forgotten that fencing is better than a travesty, and more than an amusement intended for the recreation of the idlers of the gallery.

Authors who had you as a master have adopted as a motto the proud speech of Armand Carrel who, speaking of his pen and his épée, said "I am prompt for one and ready for another."

As for the elegant men of the world who gather at your fencing sale they do not disregard the title of "Pupil of Jacob" as a mark of respect. And all the men among them manifest however a child-like diligence. A little more certain to never "receive", they absolutely hold their point "to give", reserving their liberalness for other better occasions than the ambush.

It is thus, my dear Jacob, and I wish you well, that one can say, without too much paradox, that your fencing salle is the vestibule of congress for perpetual peace.

ANATOLE DE LA FORGE

The game of the épée

Introduction

Are there two sorts of fencing? Yes.

Is everything that is possible in the fencing salle also possible on the duelling ground? No.

There are two sorts of fencing, I say, fencing for the salle and fencing for the duelling ground.

It is not that there are two sorts of attack but that there are two very different methods of applying them.

Besides, in the salle, fencing, as it is typically practiced, is all about convention. Indeed, the first convention permitted in the salle, whereas the touch of the button at the chest is all that is said to count whereas on the duelling ground everything counts, hits to the head, the arm, the hand, the leg also count as much as hits to the chest.

After another convention one must parry a frank attack instead of making an extension and, if there is a double-hit in any case, he who has extended is declared to be at fault.

"I attacked so you should have parried" as is often said in the fencing salle. On the duelling ground one extends at will and, in the case of a double-hit, each and both are equally in fault, for both have been wounded.

What's more, one often sees amateurs remark that they will never try on the duelling ground such-and-such risky attack which they would use themselves in the salle.

It is however very necessary that the surrounding conditions where one finds oneself in the two cases are very different. On the duelling ground one has less aplomb and has less ability to step or lunge. One can slip more easily especially when one has not considered the ruggedness of the ground or some sort of obstacle which risks making one fall. One does not have any sandals nor fencing attire; thus will one have less freedom of movement.

In addition the notion of distance changes when outside and this must be held in great consideration.

That is not all: on the duelling ground one typically stands in guard at a much greater distance than that made in the fencing salle, not only because the notion of distance differs but also and especially because one has in front of him a bare blade instead of a buttoned foil.

At the usual distance one will be too easily touched on the extremities.

When one stands in guard at longer distance one has less blade, one can thus only parry with the half-strong of the blade and one is thus obliged to parry with greater force.

Also certain parries used in the salle are dangerous on the duelling ground as not pushing the blade aside enough, and not allowing a good riposte without uncovering oneself or exposing one to a double-hit.

Here is a certain number of important differences between the two sorts of fencing.

As for different weights between the weapons used for the assault and the duel, that is to say the foil and the épée, it is only a slight difference which I consider negligible especially with a well-made épée that is well balanced for its weight, such as that which the adversaries should have or their witnesses must choose. In other terms what differentiates the game of the foil and the game of the épée is not the material difference in the weapons but the different conditions in which one is employed, one in conventional assaults, the other in a duel. In summary the game of the foil is synonymous with the game of the salle, the game of the épée is synonymous with the game of the duelling ground.

I do not insist any longer on the role that courage plays in the duel between the combatants; it is obvious that in front of sharpened épées and in front of the threat that comes from an un-buttoned tip and a thrusting point, courage plays a great role and can give the advantage to a very brave adversary who, when in an assault, would otherwise be at a disadvantage. But we should not consider this unusual case, we must consider the usual case where the adversaries have equal courage.

For all the reasons mentioned before are sufficient, as one has seen, to establish the great differences between fencing in the assault and that of the duelling ground, which renders necessary a special game.

For a long time, Jacob had this idea and an instinct for this game. The frequent consultations for duels that were asked of him from the beginning also contributed to his study of the duelling ground.

It is striking to see in the ordinary assaults in the fencing salle either as many double-hits as hits touching the arm, the leg or the head, blows which in the salle are said not to count but which, naturally, count like any other on the duelling ground.

Well-trained fencers who are habituated to relying on the conventions of the salle a little too much are thus touched in a duel by novice fencers especially when they, not knowing what to do, throw out their arm at every opportunity.

Sometimes these extensions aid double-hits to an open chest, Double-hits are otherwise one of the great hazards of the game of the salle.

What would be the practical usefulness of the science of fencing used on the duelling ground if it was found to not prevent the unusual and risky attacks which, too often in the fencing salle, allow a novice fencer to touch a well-practiced fencer and sometimes even train both combatants to make double-hits to the exposed chest?

These differences of each attack were studied by Jacob while fencing with a provost who was permitted to hit where he liked anywhere on the body by whatever means possible without preoccupying himself with the conventions of the fencing salle.

The experience often repeated and applied on the duelling

ground allowed Jacob to make a special practical game taking into consideration all that he encountered.

It is for this special game that I shall reveal the general principals.

Permit me to remark that a method of this type has not been published despite the numerous publications on fencing. While, on the contrary, that of fencing in the assault or the game of the foil has been well exposed in several treatises, especially those of Gomard, but the authors speak very briefly on the game of the duelling ground and even desire to, in general, to assimilate fencing for the assault with that of the duel.

Besides it is important to remark for now that, despite the differences between the two sorts of fencing, I do not wish to deny the usefulness of studying the foil, in other words the game of the salle, with regards to the duelling ground; on the contrary I say that it is an excellent preparation for becoming strong with the épée.

Thus if one has time ahead, one must make use of the foil. Indeed the attacks are the same for the épée as the foil except there is a different application and if the game of the foil is more difficult than performing the game of the épée it better facilitates learning it; he who can do more can do less.

Every strong foil fencer will become strong quickly at épée. He already knows, for a certain measure, all the attacks. It is just that he must be trained to better apply them when épée in hand; if strong at foil he must not improvise a game of the duelling ground and risk being touched by an épée fencer trained the same way but for less time.

What's more it is no less true that one cannot become strong at épée without having first had the opportunity to become strong at foil.

Indeed the foil is above all a game of performing by the rules; qualities of head and judgement are obviously necessary there but physical means play a greater role there than in épée.

It is also a great merit of the game of the épée that it is above all a game of the head where the chances can be better equalised between both adversaries of unequal physiques. By use of judgement and reason one can especially supplement for insufficiencies of a mediocre body-type.

Additionally the game of the épée offers resources even for an inexperienced combatant who has not taken many lessons before he fights.

Of these it is his inexperience which provides particular interest as the game of the épée offers a very simple tactic and supported by a number of examples.

The game certainly does not have the pretension to allow a fencer to improvise form the outset but, nevertheless, it allows a novice combatant to conduct himself suitably on the duelling ground, to overcome his adversary, to receive a less grievous wound if he is touched and, sometimes, even to hit a more experienced fencer who does not know the game of the épée.

Having made these remarks I shall expound upon the general principals of my method.

Since everything counts on the duelling ground and we are not concerned solely with hits to the chest one must aim to place, in the game of épée, hits to what I call "the advanced part". That is to say that which is closest to the tip whatever part that may be - the arm, the hand, the leg and even the head, if the adversary leans his head forward.

These attacks are represented very often as the foundation of my épée lesson; they are, in reality, only the basics before their special application. I recommend these for every inexperienced combatant.

Since blows aimed to the "advanced part" are easiest to reach with the point they are the easiest.

Besides they offer the advantage that they do not require one to lunge too far which is best avoided on the duelling ground.

Indeed one knows that it is less useful to lunge there than in the fencing salle. One can slip more easily, "pass through" the attack, being so far apart when engaged. What's more, especially for a less strong fencer, he who lunges has spent all his means and becomes disordered.

When one has lunged, it is for him a critical moment where his adversary has every advantage of the situation. Allowing your adversary to lunge, to spend all his means, and to not lunge yourself, is, as I shall reveal in detail, the principal tactic of a fencer who well-knows the game of the épée.

Attacks to the advanced part also have the advantage of avoiding double hits.

Moreover, from a point of view of defence, they markedly hinder an adversary and can stop many of his movements. The use of these simple attacks and tactics is thus impressed upon he who, on the eve of a duel, knows nothing or next-to-nothing of arms. Will you teach those in one or a few lessons on the duelling ground, which is sometimes their first lesson at arms, attacks on the lunge and complicated parries? This game when done badly will do nothing except expose them to be taken advantage of and make combat more one-sided and more dangerous.

I have shown in a general way the usefulness and principal role of these attacks. Do not bother yourself with wondering what type of wound they will cause as one must above all, when on the duelling ground, touch and not be touched.

Additionally the blow to the hand is naturally one of those which puts a man out of the fight very quickly.

That said, my method is far more than only reaching out to the advanced part by thrusting for the extremities as it teaches, on the contrary, when dealing with practiced fencers or those with time ahead of them a game with very varied attacks to the body. They are as recommended as any other method, only that they are taught in a different fashion.

For this, attacks to the hand and arm, as I shall explain insistently later on, are especially used as false attacks intended to cause the adversary to attack frankly on the lunge, thus spending himself, in such a way that it allows a parry and riposte to the body.

What's more, even for the experienced fencer, it is better on occasion to content oneself with thrusting to the advanced parts, as it does not expose oneself to be reached on the body.

In every case, that they do not use attacks to the advanced part, they must at least be wary of their adversaries. They will either take special care in their parry and riposte or in their avoidances.

Every épée fencer must take up a partly different guard from that of the foil to make avoidances more easily.

He must with greater care than at foil hold the right arm bent and bring in the elbow.

Withdrawal of the arm is necessary to parry well and to have an easier release while attacking or riposting, at the same time this allows you to more easily avoid attacks to the arm.

The same goes for bringing in the elbow with more care than the foil since, épée in hand, the adversary can aim there as well as the chest.

But especially, instead of holding the arm at an angle and across that of the adversary, as in foil, one holds the épée straight out, horizontally, to launch attacks more directly and to make it possible to reach the advanced part of the adversary, who will be well threatened, as well as to protect against those who advance upon you.

Furthermore one holds his guard at a greater distance than at foil and in such a way that the tips are barely touching.

Any closer and you will be easily touched on the extremities and, for another part, you will often give away too much blade: as, in the game of the épée, one must give less blade than in foil because it is more prudent and good to avoid so that the adversary cannot impede your weapon. Here is why one must go on guard at the distance shown. This case will be known by strong fencers, during combat, who will approach into range and under favourable conditions will thrust to the body.

As for the use of attacks to the body, the essential principle of the game of the épée is that, since very great caution is necessary on the duelling ground, one must always attack the blade, set it aside or control it before thrusting to the body.

With the result that full fledged attacks, remises, time-hits and redoubling to the body will be avoided, and that, the game of parry and riposte or counter-riposte will take a great place in my method.

As for attacking first, what is the case?

While one can make every attack in foil to the advanced part, because one stays far away and one can with a half-lunge - on the contrary one will make fewer frank attacks to the body as, on the duelling ground, it is particularly dangerous to lunge, as I have explained. It often happens with these frank attacks that one lies entirely spent without succeeding in touching as one is hampered due to the measure and the unfavourable physical conditions that one finds oneself under.

What's more even if one touches while lunging with a frank attack to the body, one strongly risks being touched himself at the same time. These double-hits are a great hazard of fencing where one must, in summary, "touch without being touched". It has been objected, it is true, that he who lunges can avoid a double-hit by means of opposition and elevation for the blade. This is not sufficient. Opposition and elevation are useful, without doubt, and I recommend them, as in foil, for every attack thru at the body; but they only allow you to protect one line, for there are at least four principal lines, or to put it better, an entire body to protect: quarte, sixte, septime and octave. It is especially difficult to predict in which line the adversary will extend or into which he will attack.

One will respond that a truly strong fencer will have the wherewithal to see the moment of departure and to know where he must oppose.

This will be seen to be very difficult for immediate attacks such as the disengage. In each case it is very risky. As such, in a reasoned method, one must proscribe every attack which can expose one to risks even when there is a great chance of success. Besides, the range of choices is not lacking in attacks, which do not expose one to risk, except those that attack the body.

For attacks to the body, I advise two that are able to protect the attacker with sufficient means.

These two attacks are the threatened croisé of seconde and the double beat finishing with a direct attack in sixte. These two well-done attacks protect the attacker because the first controls the blade; the second sets it aside violently.

I shall explain later how to perform these two attacks. Adding simply that the first is done while departing from an engagement of quarte, the second departing from an engagement of sixte; one is thus assured of being able, in one or other line or a general engagement, of making an attack to the body.

Sometimes one can be content with a single beat to then thrust to the body if the beat is fairly vigorous and it chases the adversary's blade well.

But, as a general rule it is preferable to seek out one of the two shown attacks.

If, by avoidance, the adversary does not give his épée for the beat then make much accentuated feints towards his head or false attacks to the advanced parts. This will bring him to give his blade and then one can immediately perform a double beat and thrust direct or a croisé in seconde.

These two attacks besides can be employed in diverse fashions. They are very useful in reprise attacks. What's more the double beat and the croisé, combined with certain parries, can prepare excellent ripostes or counter-ripostes.

Reprise attacks, performed immediately after a fencing phrase, often overcome an adversary who, guarding against the first impact, holds himself less well on guard or is disordered. However they succeed much better and, in summary, are very practical if one is oneself not disordered nor disrupted by the first impact.

One will then have less difficulty to hit than from a direct simple attack. But, however, despite the advantages which is often presented by a reprise of attack, I submit it to the same rules as I do for attacks; that is to say, for the advanced part, it is of no importance where one reprises the attack, but when directed to the body, a reprise of attack must not be made immediately but must always be preceded by an attack on the blade with preference to the double beat thrust direct in sixte or the croisé of seconde.

Beats and croisés can also, as I have said, be combined with certain parries and prepare excellent ripostes or counter-ripostes which have the notable advantage of preventing remises and redoublements because they can control or chase away the blade quickly.

In addition the more certain game for thrusts at the body is the game of parries and ripostes with counter-ripostes. Thus we arrive at the veritable foundation of my épée lessons.

Since, on the duelling ground, greater caution is necessary than in the salle; since the material conditions are less favourable and that, besides, the conventions are not there to protect from irregular attack, it was necessary to give a great place for ripostes and counter-ripostes in fencing for the duelling ground which, will not commit a fencer, as it is often done with an attack on the lunge, but leaves him with all his wits, and what's more, coming after one or two parries, which have chased or controlled the blade, exposing him much less, in total, to risky attacks than immediate attacks to the body. Without doubt be wary of remises, as they are dangerous for those who preform them and I proscribe them as they expose one to the double-hit.

But, for the rest, certain parries and ripostes chosen as explained, allow one to impede remises and, in total, the game of parries and ripostes or counter-ripostes is by far the most certain.

It is first important to make a choice between parries, recalling that, to have a full value, a parry must not only set aside the épée but also facilitate a riposte.

The first of these two qualities is however very necessary at épée as this game requires great authority as I will insist on many occasions.

Under penalty of not unsettling the adversary, parries must be much more accentuated in épée than in foil, because one has less blade, because one parries often with only the half-strong of the blade and because often on the duelling ground the adversary will resist instinctively with more force than in the salle against the action of a parry. While always accentuating the parry, one must avoid setting aside his épée and seek to maintain the tip in line such as to keep it always threatening, so that it protects if the parry is deceived and permits a quick return to another parry.

This can be done by holding the grip more firmly than a foil and by parrying with a crisp movement of the fingers and the thumb which will immediately stop and return the blade to be in line well.

It is not enough, as I have said, for a parry to be good and to only set aside the blade, it must also facilitate a riposte. Every parry which does not allow a convenient riposte must be rejected from the game of the épée. Additionally, if one cannot riposte, it is much better not to seek to parry but to retreat or jump back by one pace.

The step and especially the jump back, which I shall revisit, are the most certain means of avoiding a hit. If thus one cannot riposte either because one has become disordered or the adversary is too far away or looking to counter-riposte it is much better to retreat or jump backwards instead of looking to parry or simply retire your arm if the adversary's épée is not aiming for your arm or hand.

On the contrary, if one is in a good position to parry, riposte or counter-riposte do not lose the opportunity to do so while employing parries chosen as follows:

In the high line quarte and especially counter-quarte, well executed, are the best parries. They protect the whole line without risking bringing the épée toward the body as counter-sixte does and, what's more, they give a better place to riposte, which is not given by a parry of sixte. The wrist has, besides, more force in quarte than in sixte. Then, in quarte, the arm stays in front of the chest and protects the body in the case where a parry is deceived.

One performs sometimes a parry of sixte for variety; if one parries only with counter-quarte in the high line, one greatly risks aiding the adversary in deceiving the counter. Only, after the parry of sixte, the riposte to the body is not very convenient, so it will be prudent on this occasion to riposte to the advanced part.

In the low line, seconde is better than septime and octave because the hand in seconde parries better in that line with more force, the thumb placed in such a way to support the wrist. The riposte is, furthermore, easier either to the arm or to the body after a parry of seconde. The same remarks are made on the subject of counter-seconde which will be equally practical with care.

Septime will however be employed for variety sometimes with the parry of seconde

Prime and quinte are dangerous to use as they are too exposing.

Prime is, besides, difficult to perform and quinte can hardly chase the blade outside the line of the body.

On the subject of parries, let me add that one should not employ parries of contraction, because they risk bringing the adversary's épée too much into the line and they do not facilitate the riposte. In revenge, it will be very useful to complete parries in the high line either with a croisé of seconde or with beats. I insist on these type of very practical parries.

Parries being thus chosen and well practiced, an épée fencer has every advantage to avoid an attack but rather to let himself be attacked to parry and riposte. And the sooner his adversary makes a frank attack the better because he will overly commit himself and allow a very convenient riposte or counter-riposte to the body.

On the advanced part, every sort of simple or compound riposte is possible. They will be well suited to the fencers with less confidence. To the body, only direct ripostes shall be done. As for compound ripostes to the body, for the same reasons as I gave for attacks, one hardly uses them without exception.

Counter-ripostes give an additional security because they

often find an adversary disordered and confused not only by your parry but by the effort which himself made to parry-riposte. They allow you thus to arrive progressively and more certainly at the body if oneself has not become disordered.

They play, in summary a large role upon which I insist on in detail.

To become able to do this game of parries, ripostes and counter-ripostes which, as I have come to show, is the foundation of the game of the épée, one must naturally know how to make oneself be attacked, one must aid the adversary in uncovering himself and in over-committing.

To aid him in this one does not press upon him, but waits and, what's more, one uses all manner of feints.

Time matters little on the duelling ground where one needs to touch only once. Much better to be patient and assist more certainly the adversary to over-commit, without over-committing oneself.

It is not important at which body part one aims feints and false attacks and, furthermore, one makes feints not only with movements of the épée but with movements of the body.

Feints with the blade are very accentuated, as the game of the épée, I repeat, requires great authority.

Slightly hesitant feints do not disrupt an adversary but do let him see the setup you have planned; and since you are more wary on the duelling ground than in the salle the adversary will respond less to feints.

Sometimes feints are made with a movement of the body, as I shall explain in detail. Sometimes one exposes the hand or the arm for him to thrust at then parry and riposte. Every method is good on the duelling ground where one aims above all to hit only once.

One must know to make a choice between methods, use each one in turn but without hurrying; one must vary, but not multiply or complicate movements. Be sobre in your actions, this is otherwise a very important rule in the game of the épée. Every movement must be done for a reason.

Every useless action is by itself dangerous because it will furnish the adversary with some sort of preparation.

Now, to finish the general principals of the game of the épée, we must reveal the three rules relative to the execution of attacks and intended to give greater speed, aplomb and security on the duelling ground.

These rules apply to every thrust whether it is an attack, riposte or counter-riposte aimed at the chest or at the advanced part.

The first of these rules, for the épée, the attack must not be carried but "thrown".

By means of a rapid release, throw the attack then immediately withdraw the arm.

Indeed, at épée, above all, when one goes for the hit, do so as quickly as possible then return to guard no less quickly and well in line.

With a sharpened épée, if one quickly and briskly throws the attack there will be no better touch. Furthermore reaching out an attack as in foil, one will take too long to return to the defensive and will often be too exposed.

The second rule is that every épée attack, and even feints and false attacks, must be accompanied by an appel of the foot.

These appels aim to:

> 1st- give greater grounding and more aplomb on the
> duelling ground
> 2nd- more swing for throwing an attack
> 3rd- To impress the adversary, to make him think
> you are making an attack on the lunge rather than
> a simple attack on the demi-lunge which will aid
> them in over-committing.

Finally- a very important rule- after each attack to the body one must make an immediate jump backwards while recovering well on guard, point always on line.

Of course this jump must not be disordered. It is done by carrying both feet backwards at the same time, but without separation, without losing the guard position and épée well in line after each attack is thrown.

To jump back in this way is of premier importance whether one touches or not. One is not certain, indeed, of having touched and even if one has touched an injured adversary is perfectly able to riposte and even give a wound more dangerous than his own.

While jumping backwards one avoids the riposte in the most certain way and stays in a solid guard ready to parry with the blade or even attack. A simple step backwards is less rapid; furthermore it often gives less aplomb on the duelling ground, disrupting you even more.

The backwards jump is sometimes also employed when the combat turns into a bad engagement and even if there hasn't been an attacked launched or riposte to the body. If the combat is badly engaged it is much better to break apart in this way with a jump backward rather than to, as with certain fencers, do multiple movements which disrupts and leads to nothing, other than to expose you.

The jump forwards, under certain conditions which I shall show, is equally used in the game of the épée, especially in the case of a fencer of small size, as I shall explain in the special cases.

I have now achieved revealing the main core of this method: one can see that it tries to offer at once a very varied and reasoned game in all its parts, leaving nothing to chance and considering every condition which one will find on the duelling ground.

It will be good as well to practice often this game on the duelling ground: we will thus discover its practical utility. In the fencing salle one is not aware of the effects produced by nature of the ground nor the changes in the notions of distance in the open air. Furthermore in the salle one rarely has the space to step or retreat sufficiently. In a duel, as in combat, one makes steps and counter-steps.

Such are the principal rules of the game of épée.

To practice this game with success one must, as I have said, have great head and wherewithal.

The professor must facilitate this task and habituate his pupils to reason.

He must explain to them not only the manner of performing these attacks, not only the how but also the why of these attacks.

He must explain why such a blow exposes one to risk, why this blow must be done at such a moment or on such an occasion. One must learn to make this occasion part of your nature. It is your adversary who you must let you thrust, who must provide you the opportunity and a foreseen opportunity.

Furthermore, it is important not to thrust in a hurry, but to thrust correctly, otherwise said one must govern one's speed and thrust accordingly while profiting from the preparations or the steps from the adversary.

Then I repeat that one must vary the game as much as possible but while avoiding useless actions. One must rather wait, watching those of the adversary, not only to impede his position but also to profit from his smallest mistakes.

Now that the principals of the game of the épée are presented in a general fashion, let us see how to study them practically.

I will determine this matter with several cases, because my method does not have absolutes.

For those special cases who, on the eve of a duel, have little or no practice of arms, I will indicate which part must be chosen from the game of the épée.

For those who, in the fencing salle, have acquired a certain ability with the foil and understand, as a consequence, all the fencing terms and even which attacks to apply on the duelling ground- under the reserve that they must be applied in a different fashion- for these, I divide the game of the épée into eight principal lessons: though it goes without saying, of course, that eight lessons will be sufficient to possess the method.

It is for clarity to better make the progression of the steps of the game of the épée, that I adopt this division into eight principal lessons. A similar division as has been adopted in certain foil treatises, which do not have greater pretension than I in teaching weapons in a few lessons.

In addition I only give a simple overview of the method. I show only the principal applications without wishing to enumerate all of the attacks, as this will be too fastidious and in fact unhelpful.

Once we know how to apply the attacks of the foil to the épée, one should relate himself, to complete this method, to a well done foil treatise, such as that by Gomard for example.

First Lesson

Guard position-Grip-Notions on measure, steps and counter-steps- Appels-Jumps-Attacks upon the advanced part from an engagement in quarte- Parry of counter-quarte- Direct riposte to the chest.

Guard Position- For the épée, as with the foil, one naturally begins by working on the guard and grip. A well-formed guard is an essential condition in order to be strong in one or other game.

I have previously briefly shown just how different the épée guard is. One rule which does not change in both cases is that one must have an upright body, great aplomb, be well grounded and balanced on one's legs, and the haunches bent in such a way as to provide freedom and ease of movement. However, it is even more important for the duel, more so than for the assault in the salle, to move with steps and counter-steps.

One must thus step and retreat quickly without hindrance.

As with the foil hold the head upright, eyes watching the adversary and his movements.

At the same time hold the right hand at the height of the right breast, the left hand in the air, serving as a balance.

There is no need to adjust the position of the right hand under the pretext of allowing for the adversary's height. The position of the right hand at the breast is, in effect, the only way in which allows one to make well-formed parries in all lines.

The hand and nails are slightly turned upwards holding the grip more tightly than one does with a foil. This is often necessary, as has been explained, as a result of the parries which are made with the épée being greater than the foil.

In effect, as one usually has less blade contact, one can only just parry than with the half-strong of the blade.

What's more, when duelling, one often has an affair with an adversary who instinctively resists with greater force in his parrying action than when in the salle.

Hold, with greater care than with the foil, the arm bent so that it will be able to parry more freely, to have a greater release with which to attack and riposte, and also to give away less blade and better avoid touches to the arm. The elbow will be held carefully well tucked in for this last reason.

As to the direction of the point, instead of lying at an angle like a foil, I have said before that it must be held straight out, in a line, in order to launch touches directly and to be able to reach all the advanced parts of the adversary possible, which will be well threatened, and no less to protect one's own parts that are out in front.

In order to have greater certainty in the duel come on guard with the left foot moving to the rear to avoid a surprise.

Notions on measure- Once the pupil is placed on guard, the professor puts himself in turn on guard opposite him at the correct distance.

At this distance, with the épée straight out, one does not engage points along which he could guide his blade.

What's more, unless the adversary takes one step, one is protected from touches to the body and one can only be touched on the arm, even if the adversary makes a lunge.

One is in good position to make touches to the advanced parts of the adversary while still able to take advantage of an engagement, a fencing phrase to protect oneself and thrust to the body.

The correct measure taken, the professor makes careful observations as to its advantages and recommends that it is maintained as much as possible throughout the combat, except when he sees the opportunity to approach without danger.

Steps and Counter-steps- A duel, as a combat, is paced in steps and counter-steps.

One must practice to adjust one's step.

When stepping forward it is prudent to make little steps.

To retreat a little, which must be done often to avoid being touched, take much larger steps but not without exaggeration and without breaking the combat in each instance. One must get accustomed to retreat as necessary, taking great care, as it is often necessary to retreat in order to avoid being touched. It is also necessary to know, on occasion, to stay firm so as to riposte effectively to the body at proper reach. Even when the adversary steps forward one must know to not break distance instantly and sometimes, on the contrary, take advantage of this step to attack, because it will contribute to his disorder. Or the least one could adjust with a half-retreat.

Moreover, in the course of these lessons, stepping and counter-stepping exercises will be constantly blended with the principles of the touches as they are taught.

Jumps- In order to vary your steps and as a result of the duelling ground one may find oneself on, sometimes one will use little jumps forwards and backwards.

Jumps, in the épée game, have a special significance. As I have said before they are not disorganised movements. The jump that I mean is made by, in one action, carrying both feet forward or backward, but without disorder or losing one's guard position.

The term "jump" is perhaps a little too strong to describe this action, especially the forward spring, which must be made very carefully and without advancing too far. However I shall retain the term in order to avoid using excessive circumlocution.

Recall that the jump, as I mean it, offers diverse important advantages.

There is less risk of sliding on the duelling ground when springing rather than stepping.

What's more the jump is faster than the step. From this point of view, the backward jump is very useful, and as I have said, it is the most certain way to avoid a riposte or counter-riposte after a well-made touch. Also the professor must frequently make him spring backwards and always after a touch made to the body. It is strongly recommended that the pupil stays on guard so as to not become disorganised and to hold his point straight out.

Forward jumps are especially of great utility to shorter fencers, as will be explained later. They are even useful for taller fencers if they have an affair against an adversary who retreats too much.

Appels with the foot- I have shown the utility of appels in order to give greater aplomb, greater style and greater authority from which to launch touches on the duelling ground. They give a firmer point and help to quickly release an attack or riposte.

The frequent use of appels with the foot completes the practice of stepping and counter-stepping.

Attacks on the advanced part- There follows, in the first lesson, a study of the simplest touches, that is to say attacks on the advanced part. One makes them from the engagement of quarte. Make all types of touches, such as direct thrusts with absence of blade, disengagements, beat disengagements, one-two, cutovers, doubles, &c., while aiming at the advanced part, or whatever else; the head, if the adversary tilts it forward, the arm, the hand or the leg but most often is the hand and arm.

These are all done this way, the exception to this is when one thrusts at the leg, because touches to the leg are likely to lean the head forward and expose the body.

Launching touches to the advanced part, the arm for preference, one need only half-lunge as this will be sufficient to hit. When one lunge fully one often risks missing one's mark.

What's more, it is known that this is more dangerous to make a full lunge on the duelling ground than in the salle.

All of these touches must be accompanied with an appel of the foot and should be executed firstly while stood still, then while stepping, then while retreating or jumping.

The professor commands, for example:

Engage in quarte.

Disengage to his hand, at the same time appel with the foot.

On guard quickly, regain the engagement of quarte; disengage to the arm, at the same time appel with the foot. On guard.

One small step forward.

Disengage to the hand, making an appel with the foot.

On guard quickly.

Return to engagement in quarte.

Retreat with a small step.

With absence of blade thrust direct inside the arm.

On guard.

One step forward.

Disengage to the arm, with appel of the foot. On guard quickly.

I lean my head forward. Thrust direct to the head, spring backwards. On guard quickly.

In order to give greater authority to these touches one can often accompany them with beats which are important parts of the épée game, because they push aside or shake the blade and thus give greater effectiveness and authority to attacks. Only they must be made rapidly and sharply in order to make sure that a *derobement* is not used against them.

So one will make beats in quarte, disengages to the hand, beats by changing to engagement in sixte, thrust in the hand or sometimes the head and, with exception, the leg.

Move next to doubles in the hand which must be frequently alternated with disengaging beats or beats with a direct thrust.

Cutovers or one-two-threes in the hand or the arm, from an engagement of quarte, also sometimes find their use.

Then one practises trumping the engagement or the beat, always to the advanced part.

Practice these different exercises at first stood still, then stepping or retreating.

37

Parry of counter-quarte - riposte direct to the chest- Next practice to parry counter-quarte and riposte direct to the chest.

I have insisted on the essential usefulness of counter-quarte which is the best parry, as it protects all lines very well, lets the grip take all the strain and keeps the arm in front of the chest in order to cover this part if the parry fails. What's more it allows one to riposte with ease.

When performing counter-quarte, as with all the other parries, parry more vigorously than with the foil because there is less blade and also because the épée game requires greater authority.

Recall, moreover, one must, while parrying, avoid taking the épée off-line, and seek to maintain a straight point, in line, in such a way that it is always threatening and able to return very quickly to a second parry, if the first is deceived.

After a parry of counter-quarte, practice the direct riposte to the body. This riposte, as all thrusts to the body, must be done in opposition, in such a way as to cover you.

While launching the riposte one will often make an appel of the foot. As soon as the touch is launched, spring backwards.

The professor will command, for example:

Engage in quarte, I disengage over, parry counter-quarte, riposte to the chest with an appel of the foot and spring backwards.

On guard, the point well in line and well sitting on one's legs.

Practice parrying and riposting thus, interweaving these exercises with steps and counter-steps.

Second Lesson

Attacks to the advanced part from an engagement of sixte – Redoubles - Parry of quarte and counter-quarte - Ripostes after these parries - Parry of sixte and ripostes - Reprise of attacks upon the advanced part.

First perform, from an engagement in sixte, all types of attack upon the most advanced parts.

Thus the professor will command, in turn, direct touches, one-twos &c. to the hand or arm, beats thrust straight to the hand or the arm, or sometimes to the head- if the adversary leans his head- and by exception to the leg; beats, one-twos to the hand or arm; beats in quarte by changing engagement by disengaging around the advanced part; beats feinted in seconde and thrust to the arm.

Of course I am only demonstrating the principal touches.

Redoubles- Next practice redoubles to the hand or arm. These are the only redoubles that I advise; the others to the body are far too dangerous and too exposed to a double touch.

Redoubles are made against an adversary who does not riposte or who ripostes too late. They can be mixed with beats.

The professor commands, for example:

Engage in quarte. Disengage to the hand or arm, I do not riposte, redouble while staying in a half-lunge.

Disengage to the hand or arm, I do not riposte, beat in sixte and launch two touches in sixte with the épée to the hand or arm.

If the adversary not only doesn't riposte but also withdraws his arm after the first attack, redouble when he returns his arm to the fore.

In addition, if he wishes to ensure that he does not expose himself to redoubles he must become accustomed to riposte more often, at least a demi-riposte, if he fears to commit himself.

39

Parry of quarte and counter-quarte- Next practice parrying quarte or counter-quarte or one another.

To do this the professor attacks the pupil and commands: Engage in sixte, if I disengage in quarte, parry quarte, riposte direct and jump backwards. Engage in quarte, if I disengage in sixte, parry counter-quarte, riposte direct and jump backwards.

Thus one alternates between the parry of quarte and that of counter-quarte.

Then to practice parrying quarte and counter-quarte, the professor commands:

Engage in sixte; I attack with a one-two over the arm, parry quarte and counter-quarte, riposte to the chest, jump backwards.

After the parry of quarte, also make a very practical compound riposte, a riposte disengaging to the hand or the arm without lunging.

Parade of sixte and ripostes- Next practice the parade of sixte, it is less useful than quarte and counter-quarte but it is useful to use it from time to time to add variety.

If one has a parry that is used all the time the adversary will be more able to beat it.

Only, as it has less force to push aside the épée in sixte than when in quarte, as it leaves you open to be exploited, and it is less well-placed for a riposte to the body. One must be contented to thrust only at the advanced part after a parry of sixte.

The professor will command, for example:

Engage in quarte, I disengage in sixte, parry sixte, riposte to the arm or the advanced part, as you wish.

One will sometimes parry in counter-quarte, sometimes in sixte, with the ripostes as shown. It is good to thus alternate between these two parries.

In addition, after ripostes to the arm, it is not necessary to spring backwards; only to be ready to parry with counter-quarte as a safety measure in case the adversary makes a counter-riposte.

Reprise-attack- Next practice some very simple reprise attacks, aimed at the advanced part.

Reprise attacks are one of the most practical resources for a fencer who is not overwhelmed by a lively phrase in combat.

In such cases a novice fencer remains in a less solid guard, perhaps even freezing as if the combat has been interrupted, and, in summary, is not ready to parry a new attack which he may not even notice.

The professor commands, for example;

Engage in sixte.

I disengage in quarte, parry quarte, riposte direct, I parry quarte and do not counter-riposte; return to guard and quickly make one or two touches with the épée to the arm.

Often, when landing a hit from a reprise attack, it won't even require much speed; proper timing is more important.

I shall speak later on reprise-attacks to the body.

Third Lesson

Low line - Parries of seconde, counter-seconde and septime -Ripostes after these parries - Parries of seconde and sixte, of seconde and quarte - Ripostes after these parries - Ripostes with a redouble to the arm - Withdrawing the arm or leg - Stop-thrusts to the head.

In the third lesson we are first concerned with touches to the low line, especially the means by which to parry them.

As for attacks to the low line I often advise croisé of seconde of which I shall speak later. Apart from croisés one will almost only do feints to the low line, because one risks exposing too much and receiving a touch to the face or chest.

Of the parries, which I have demonstrated before, the best for the low line are the seconde and counter-seconde. The hand has more strength and authority in the seconde position as the thumb secures the grip; what's more, the riposte is easier after these parries than from after septime. However practice parrying septime for variety, and then riposte at the advanced part.

Fencers more used to the sabre will also, on occasion, parry low prime, which is done in the same hand position as seconde only in the other line.

To parry seconde, or counter-seconde, turn the nails underneath but without lowering the arm or lowering the point to the ground as is done by some fencers.

On the contrary parry sharply, without quitting the blade, and keep the point on line.

After a parry of seconde or counter-seconde one sometimes ripostes in the low line.

But more often one ripostes to the chest by disengaging to the chest, or advanced part, which, most often, will be the arm.

Alternate between both types of riposte.

A riposte to the chest will be used when a parry of seconde

has been strongly made and the adversary is disorganised.

The professor will command, for example;

I disengage to the low line, parry seconde and riposte to the arm or riposte to the chest and spring back.

Before riposting to the arm, you will be best to retreat a little while parrying, because if you are too close your aim for the arm will be off and you risk "overshooting" it. Also to say, moreover, that after any parry, seconde or otherwise, if one wishes to riposte to the arm it is often useful to retreat slightly while parrying, then riposte while stood still.

Suppose now that a parry of seconde has been deceived. Most often it will be deceived in the high line; one must therefore parry seconde and quarte or seconde and sixte.

The professor commands, for example:

I threaten the low line then I disengage to the high line, parry seconde and quarte (1) riposte to the chest and spring back.

I threaten the low line then I disengage to the high line, parry seconde and sixte, riposte to the arm.

Alternate between both of these games of parrying.

If the parry of seconde is deceived in the low line one must parry seconde and counter-seconde then riposte to the arm or the chest.

Ripostes with a redouble to the arm- After the different parries shown for the high line and low line, now practice riposting with a redouble to the arm, using the conditions explained before for redoubling an attack, that's to say if the adversary does not riposte or ripostes too slow.

(1) This is often called a "half-counter" of quarte which is done in each case; but the term "half-counter" is rarely used.

Withdrawing the arm or leg- Do not always look to parry as has been shown: It is useless and sometimes even dangerous, if one does not riposte or would have to make a parry which would be easily deceived. It is better to jump back if you are in a bad engagement, surprised or too disorganised to make a good parry or riposte.

Instead of springing backwards content oneself, on occasion, with withdrawing the arm when the adversary's épée is only aimed at the arm or hand. Only be wary of redoubles and always be ready to avoid or parry and riposte.

Alternate between this game of avoiding a touch and ordinary parries.

In summary one will sometimes parry touches to the hand or arm with ordinary parries, sometimes avoid them by withdrawing the arm and retreating a little way while ready to avoid redoubles or parry them.

To avoid touches to the leg it is sufficient to sometimes withdraw the leg instead of a parry of seconde or septime and riposte. Every time you withdraw the leg threaten or thrust at the head at the same time. Be especially wary that the adversary is not making a false attack, precisely intended to provoke a threat or a touch to the head in order to seize your blade and thrust to the body.

For the remainder, throw a threat or a touch and withdraw the arm while also returning to guard backwards.

Stop-thrusts to the head- Stop-thrusts have, above all, a use against an adversary who charges or those who either attack to the legs or wide off the line of the body. In general those who charge tilt their head forward and hold their arm back and threaten the low line.

As soon as we see him rush in thrust to the head and spring back.

I do not advise a stop-thrust to anywhere other than the head. Trying a stop-thrust to the chest risks a double hit. This danger does not exist for the head, under the conditions shown, and furthermore head hits have greater authority than any other and are better at stopping an adversary; he will return naturally to the ordinary parry instead of continuing his attack. To perform a stop-thrust, thrust straight out in front of you, with an appel of the foot or a half-lunge then jump back.

The stop-thrust can be done as a direct touch if the adversary does not beat nor change engagement. If he does avoid the blade and thrust at the head, then spring back.

Suppose that the stop-thrust does not touch the adversary and that he continues to charge: parry, while retreating, quarte and counter, or seconde and counter, or septime or sometimes low prime until you have regained the adversary's blade. Then stop in order to riposte quickly while stood still then spring back.

If, after you have parried and riposted, you don't hit him and the adversary continues his pursuit try a new stop-thrust and then resume the parries shown; alternate between stop-thrusts, parries and ripostes.

Fourth Lesson

Attacks to the body - Double beats direct thrust from an engagement of sixte; threatened croisé in seconde, from an engagement in quarte - The use of these thrusts in reprise attacks - Parries of double counter-quarte, counter-quarte and sixte, counter-quarte and seconde or septime- Parries following beats or cross - ripostes after these various parries.

I have explained before why I do not recommend attacks aiming for the body.

On the duelling ground where is it particularly dangerous to lunge without having controlled or gained the épée, or where the conditions underfoot are not favourable and where, commonly, one is engaged at a fair distance, so that one will not be able to reach often using an attack to the body, due to being fully engaged, or to touch him without success to not be touched oneself as, more or less, one risks getting a touch for giving a touch. As a consequence, as I have posited, as the essential principle, is that one must first attack the blade, push it aside or control his blade before attacking the body. Moreover, I have expressed a preference for two thrusts which particularly protect the attacker and which are, from an engagement of quarte, the threatened croisé of seconde and, from an engagement of sixte, a double beat and direct thrust.

Now see how to perform these two touches.

To threaten in croisé, command:

Engage in quarte and earnestly threaten the head while tapping your foot, cross the épée swiftly into seconde, lunge, recover in quarte without quitting his blade and spring back.

A threat to the head often has greater effect than one to the chest, épée in hand, when intended to upset an adversary, then seize the épée, strong to weak, in order to make an effective croisé.

It must be done earnestly, and with opposition (1)

For a double beat thrust direct, command:

Engage in sixte, make two beats, one in quarte as the point flies in, the second in sixte, more violent, as a pressure, while holding the point straight out directly at the chest, lunge and spring back.

The first beat is made more softly so that the adversary will have less expectation of a violent attack which will come with the second beat.

The second beat, very vigorous, must completely free the way and allow a thrust to the body before the adversary's épée can return on line.

Repeat these two essential touches for a long time and with great care as explained.

Sometimes these are done while stood still, other times while stepping or breaking measure.

What's more, one can perform these on the preparation or upon the step of the adversary.

It is thus where it has the greatest chance of success.

It must therefore be performed often, alternated with attacks to the advanced part to vary the game.

To succeed with the threatened croisé of seconde or the double beat thrust direct from sixte against an adversary who do not offer up his blade, one must make false attacks at him at his advanced part, or threaten his head which will encourage him to make an engagement in the high line. As soon as he takes a quarte or sixte launch with swiftness.

Command, for example: I do not offer up my blade, make threats to my head, I take engagement of quarte, make a threat of croisé in second and spring back.

---

(1) If one encounters too much resistance from the adversary when you wish to make a croisé complete the touch by a disengagement of the arm.

47

One can precede the double beat and the croisé in second with a false attack, while disengaging for example.

The professor commands: Engage in quarte, disengage the hand with a half-feint, I do not parry and stay in line, make a double beat, without rising up, thrust direct to the body while completing a lunge, and spring back.

If you find yourself too far away, after having disengaged, you will have to bring up the left foot while making two beats.

Command equally: Take an engagement of quarte, and half-disengage to the hand, I do not parry and stay on line, return in quarte, croisé of seconde without pause, lunge and spring back.

Moreover one can, after having disengaged, bring up the left foot to make a better hit of the croisé of seconde.

The double beat direct thrust and the croisé can also form an excellent reprise attack.

As reprise attacks these two thrusts can greatly unsettle an adversary who is already disordered by a lively phrase; thus they will be done with greater authority.

Take as an example, the professor commands: Take an engagement of sixte; I disengage in quarte, parry quarte, riposte direct, I parry and do not counter-riposte, return to guard and re-launch yourself while making the double beat, or the croisé of seconde.

Other than the double beat direct thrust and threatened croisé, one can also, with exception, make attacks to the chest after a single beat, if it is very vigorous and if one has upset the adversary fully. It is thus that a beat in quarte or on seconde can, on occasion, serve as sufficient preparation for an attack to the body.

The professor will command for example:

I present my blade in the high line, push aside the épée vigorously with a beat in quarte. Thrust direct to the chest and spring back.

I present my blade in the low line, push aside the épée with a beat of seconde, thrust to the body and spring back.

But these attacks to the body after a single beat must be made infrequently and with great caution.

Next practice parries of double counter-quarte, counter-quarte and sixte, counter-quarte and seconde or septime, all while parrying with greater authority than with the foil, but without making overly large movements, and while ensuring, as much as possible, that the point is out straight and in line.

Recall that one does not make parries with a contraction, because they can bring the opponent's épée in line and do not facilitate a riposte.

It is much better, what's more, to never make two consecutive parries with the épée.

I know, in effect, that this game requires a great soberness of movement; with too many movements one is exposed to risk, one risks being disorganised and furnishing the adversary with an opportunity to prepare. From these one will often find a route or play through these numerous movements. It is better to take an opportunity to separate from the fight.

When one makes two consecutive parries the latter is often made while retreating in order to ensure safety. In fact it is good to parry sometimes while retreating as it gives a certain confidence to the adversary and has the advantage of surprise when one then parries with a firm foot.

The professor will thus alternate between double parries while stood still, and while retreating. Sometimes even one will parry while stepping with a small step and while breaking measure.

Only always parry in this way against false attacks. The adversary who attacks without intent to touch will be more surprised by a parry made while stepping, especially when one has retreated two or three times before. But, one must, naturally, redouble one's attention and caution fully in order to allow oneself to parry while stepping, or when breaking measure, even so that the adversary has not attacked fully.

To practice these various games of parrying the professor commands, for example:

Engage in quarte: I one-two inside, parry sixte and quarte while retreating, riposte direct on the lunge, spring back.

Engage in quarte: I one-two on the half- lunge, parry sixte and quarte while making a small step or while gathering measure, riposte direct on the lunge, spring back.

Take an engagement of quarte, I double in sixte, parry counter-quarte and sixte stood still, riposte to the arm.

Repeat following the same attack and the same parries, but, this time, I recommend retreating while parrying.

The professor commands, again, for example:

Engage in quarte: I disengage in sixte to double, while deceiving again your counter-quarte in the high line, this time taking the double counter-quarte while retreating with a small step, riposte direct to the body and spring back.

Engage in quarte: I double on the half-lunge in the high line, parry double counter-quarte while making a small step or gaining measure, riposte direct and spring back.

Engage in quarte. I double while deceiving your counter-quarte in the low line, parry counter-quarte and seconde while retreating, riposte to the arm.

I repeat the same attack; this time staying still while parrying seconde, riposte to the chest and spring back.

To complete the parries in the high line it will often be useful to use the croisé of seconde or beats.

For example, after having parried counter-quarte, make a lively croisé of seconde while well controlling the blade.

Or it is good to parry quarte with a flying point and then make a vigorous beat-expulsion in sixte, then thrust direct to the chest.

For the reasons given before on the matter of attacks to the body, the double beat and croisé of seconde are intended to push a side the adversary's blade and disorder him. In summary, they open a route to the body with as much safety as possible. What's more, these actions are excellent for breaking the line and for ending a phrase, which will be dangerous to stay in for too long. If, for example, one sees that an adversary is wary of the counter-riposte, or he himself seeks to counter-riposte, it is better to stop this phrase by accompanying a parry with a croisé and beats while thrusting to the body.

Fifth Lesson

Direct counter-ripostes

I have spoken previously of the importance of counter-ripostes in the épée game.

Well done, they often disrupt an adversary at the beginning of a fencing phrase and unsettle him, not only with the parry which gains his épée but also by the effort which he must make to parry and riposte.

The counter-riposte thus allows one to arrive progressively and with greater certainty to the body, if one knows how not to disorganise himself.

One can cite a great number of direct and compound counter-ripostes.

I shall simply give a taster of the principles, the more practical ones, starting with the simplest.

These consist of making a false attack at the advanced part, such as a disengagement, a beat-disengagement or one-two to the arm, to encourage the adversary to parry and riposte, in order that one can parry him and counter-riposte directly to the chest. Jump back immediately.

Here, for example, are some elementary counter-ripostes which should be learned thoroughly.

The professor commands:

Engage the épée in quarte, demi-disengage to the arm, I parry counter-quarte and riposte direct, parry quarte and counter-riposte to the chest. Spring back.

Engage the épée in quarte, disengage to the hand, I parry sixte and riposte direct. Take counter-quarte and counter-riposte direct. Spring back.

Take an engagement of sixte, make a false attack, a one-two to the arm, I parry quarte and sixte and riposte direct. Take counter-quarte and counter-riposte to the chest. Spring back.

One can equally parry sixte upon the adversary's riposte. After this parry one must commonly counter-riposte to the advanced part and sometimes to the body.

The professor commands, for example:

Engage in sixte, make a false attack, a one-two to the arm, I parry quarte and sixte and riposte direct. Parry sixte and counter-riposte to the arm. Immediately repeat the same action while making a counter-riposte to the body.

I shall now include a composed counter-riposte found to be of very great use.

The professor commands:

Engage the épée in quarte, disengage at the hand, I parry sixte and riposte underneath. Parry seconde and counter-riposte to the arm or chest, spring back.

Let us add when one counter-ripostes to the advanced part, lunging is useless, it is much better to not lunge or only a little; one will make a better touch at this distance.

After practicing these fairly simple counter-ripostes we shall move on to more difficult direct counter-ripostes.

The professor commands, for example:

Take an engagement of quarte. I thrust at the hand or I demi-disengage in the line of sixte, take counter-quarte, demi-riposte, I parry quarte and riposte direct, re-parry quarte, counter-riposte on the lunge and spring back.

Take an engagement of sixte, I disengage in quarte, parry quarte, demi-riposte, I parry quarte and riposte direct, re-parry quarte, counter-riposte on the lunge and spring back.

I thrust in the low line, parry seconde, riposte to the arm, I parry sixte and riposte direct, re-take counter-quarte, counter-riposte to the chest.

I thrust in the low line, parry seconde, if I deceive this parry in the high line return to quickly parry quarte or sixte, riposte on the half-lunge to parry quarte or counter-quarte and counter-riposte to the chest.

Take an engagement of sixte.

I disengage in quarte, parry quarte, riposte underneath, on the half-lunge, so that I parry seconde and riposte over the top, re-parry quarte or sixte and counter-riposte on the lunge.

Other useful counter-ripostes:

The professor commands, for example:

Take an engagement of sixte. I wish to change engagement or beat in quarte, deceive the change of engagement or beat by a demi-thrust to the arm, I parry sixte and riposte direct, take counter-quarte and counter-riposte on the lunge, then spring back.

Take an engagement of quarte. I wish to change engagement or beat in sixte, deceive the change of engagement or the beat while threatening a half-lunge to the chest, I parry quarte and riposte direct, re-parry quarte and counter-riposte to the chest.

Equally one can sometimes make second counter-ripostes. In other words, if the adversary parries your counter-riposte and counter-ripostes himself, you can, in turn, parry his counter-riposte and send him a second.

Thus one can make up very long phrases, with double or even triple counter-ripostes.

But these very long phrases are not to be expected when épée is in hand: they sometimes result in risky touches, and it is better to break them, either by jumping back, or by breaking the line with croisé of seconde and double beats thrust direct in sixte.

Sixth Lesson

Compound ripostes and counter-ripostes

Every touch can be made as a compound riposte at the advanced part without lunging or half-lunging.

I have explained previously some elementary compound ripostes, such as a riposte while disengaging to the arm after a parry of quarte or counter-quarte; a riposte, while disengaging to the arm or even the chest, after a parry of seconde.

One must complete these compound ripostes just as they are taught for the foil, but with the following reservations:

One can riposte to the advanced part in many ways, by disengaging, with a one-two, with a cut-over, while deceiving the counters.

But, if one thrusts to the body, one will rarely do better than, as a compound riposte, to disengage to the chest after a parry of seconde. As a general rule any other compound riposte aimed at the body will expose oneself to remises and double-hits.

On the contrary, for counter-ripostes, since the adversary is often found to be disorganised and upset by this start of the fencing phrase, one can make compound counter-ripostes even to the body.

They will be done preferably while disengaging or by deceiving counter-parades.

On the advanced parts, one can make all sorts of compound counter-ripostes.

Seventh Lesson

Feints combined with various actions

The game of the épée is, above all, as said, a game of reason, a game of the head where the good execution is not secondary.

All types of feint and all sorts of traps must be used. Especially as one must always protect oneself with great care I advise only the strongest fencer to use the feints taught in this lesson.

With these feints one seeks to deceive the adversary, as much with body actions as with épée actions; one must pretend to be uncovered and allow a part to become exposed, such as an arm, a leg, then encourage the adversary to thrust fully in order to allow yourself to parry and riposte within proper distance. In order to give them greater confidence, retreat as required a few times in a row. Sometimes step forward in order to feign exposing oneself or simply to vary the game. Accompany these various actions with feints of the épée, or better alternate between these two sorts of tricks. In one word, by any means possible, encourage the adversary to commit himself within distance of your point, without committing yourself. I repeat that this game requires good talent with the épée.

As an example of the sort of feints the professor will practice these in particular:

Engage in sixte, invite with an absence of blade to the left, exposing the hand and fore-arm for the adversary to thrust at, then you parry sixte or counter-quarte and riposte.

Engage in quarte, invite with an absence of blade to the right so that the adversary thrusts direct, then parry quarte, riposte direct and spring back.

Make this feint sometimes when stood still, sometimes while stepping or retreating.

Accompanied with these absences of blade, one will sometimes make appels of the foot, which contribute to disrupt the adversary.

Other examples:

Engaged in quarte, threaten the high line, while exposing the line underneath so that he thrusts there, and then parry second and riposte to the arm or the chest. Jump back in the latter case.

When in sixte, make a feint in the low line while exposing the arm, so that the adversary thrusts there, parry quarte or sixte and riposte.

When engaged in quarte or sixte make an absence of blade, while tilting the head to the fore, so that he thrusts there, then parry quarte and riposte. Sometimes croisé in seconde, after having parried quarte, or, better, parry quarte with a flying point in order to then make a beat-expulsion in sixte and thrust direct.

To accentuate the feint one can, all the while tilting the head to the fore, make a feint in the low line instead of a simple absence of blade. The adversary will be more inclined to thrust or to threaten in the high line. Of course these feints must be done with great care.

One can also advance the leg so he'll thrust there, then parry seconde and riposte or, better, withdraw the leg and make a stop-thrust to the head. Though it is better to parry seconde and riposte.

It is useful to combine the feints I have shown with pressures, beats and changes of engagement.

For example, when engaged in quarte, one will press very hard in quarte while exposing the arm for the adversary to disengage against, quickly parry counter-quarte and riposte to the chest, then spring back.

If the adversary does not respond to the first pressure, one will use several variations, while gradually accentuating or diminishing the action, in order to better encourage the disengagement.

All the same, one will make beats or changes of engagement or feints with a croisé with the intention to encourage the adversary to deceive them in order to then parry and riposte.

Sometimes one will only riposte on the half-lunge in order to avoid a counter-riposte on the lunge.

If the adversary does not at first respond to the feints then progressively accentuate them while increasing the length of the changes of engagement little by little, or by making beats that are a little larger.

One can even make double engagements while advancing with small steps, still for the same objective to make him trump the engagements in order to parry and riposte.

These diverse feints and the methods of varying them, by progressive accentuation, require, I repeat, very great care and a fairly good talent at the épée. While doing these one must be wary of over-exposing oneself and also making too many movements. One must know how to vary one's game, all the while avoiding unnecessary actions.

In addition if the adversary does not respond to one or other of these type of feints one must not dwell upon feints but know to change tactics. Make, for variety, false attacks against him. Thus alternate between the feints shown and these false attacks against the advanced part. If he still does not respond, one must know, on occasion, to stop, lie in wait and sometimes even refuse the blade.

On the contrary if he responds to your feints or false attacks one must then be wary that he does not seek to counter-riposte.

This is why; if one has affair against a strong adversary it is better to simply focus on ripostes at the advanced part, as this does not facilitate a counter-riposte.

Eighth lesson

Method for combating certain unorthodox games.
Advice on Smaller fencers

An épée fencer must know how to combat every game. Especially as on the duelling ground everything is allowed, except that which is dishonourable. The rules are not there, as in the fencing salle, to determine which hits are invalid. Therefore the game of épée must prepare for many kind of thrusts and give methods for combating unorthodox fencers or, more accurately, those who play out of the rules and thus depart from ordinary fencing.

I have spoken before in the third lesson as to what one does when an adversary throws himself forward with a bent arm. In such cases, one must alternate, as I have explained, between stop-thrusts to the face and parries of quarte and counter-quarte, or seconde and counter-seconde, or septime and sometimes low prime, while retreating, followed by ripostes while stood still.

Against an adversary who constantly holds his arm outstretched, while stiffening it, I have equally explained that the game to use, very simply, consists of double-beats or croisés which push aside or control the blade.

Now consider the other unorthodox games.

What to do about an adversary who refuses his blade?

One must then sometimes make false attacks on the nearest part, sometimes overly-accentuated feints to the face in order to force the adversary to come to an engagement, parry or attack, while readying oneself to parry and riposte or counter-riposte. While making these feints to the head one must be wary that the adversary does not thrust at your hand or fore-arm: if he thrusts there, parry seconde or septime and riposte sometimes to the body, sometimes to the nearest part.

Other fencers multiply beats or changes of engagement. This game does not always have the same aim: Sometimes the adversary does this frankly to unsettle you, sometimes on the contrary he seeks to encourage you to deceive his beats or changes of engagement so as to be able to parry and riposte himself.

To correctly know his intention, one must always at first make false attacks, deceive his beats or changes of engagement by demi-actions; if the adversary goes directly to the parry and riposte then one goes to counter-riposte.

If, on the contrary, the adversary does not quickly go to parry and riposte, if his intention is to only unsettle you with his beats and changes of engagement, one must deceive them frankly, and thrust only to the advanced parts.

Certain fencers seek to go *corps-a-corps*. One says also that on the duelling ground that *corps-a-corps* is for inexperienced fencers a means of equalising the odds against a more experienced fencer. To equalise chances, that's to say, but it is certain that in *corps-a-corps* fencing becomes more of a wrestling match with a weapon hand.

In addition wrestling creates most often, and more than necessary, opportunities for serious misconduct which will be returned to when discussing the questions concerning the duel. I shall say then that it is better to agree during the pre-duel discussion that the witnesses will separate the adversaries in the case of *corps-a-corps*.

But this convention is not always accepted and one must also know how to combat all of these games.

The first thing to advise, naturally, is to avoid the adversary closing to *corps-a-corps* by always being ready to give him a stop-thrust or a parry and riposte.

If he enters *corps-a-corps* I do not advise a trained fencer to stay in this range for a long time, or even seek to touch him, as he will not have many practiced means to parry and riposte nor for attacking.

Opposition with the left hand may be useful in some cases, but in general it is proscribed in a duel, often because it gives temptation to seize the épée with the hand rather than simply pushing it aside.

Since one loses his means in *corps-a-corps,* it is much better during this to not seek to thrust, because one will be exposed to a double hit.

Do not even try to make downward thrusts like a dagger blow even though using them may be tempting in such circumstances. It is much better to only seek to avoid the adversary's touches by using any means possible, such as opposing your épée against his own, and, to make it easier, to be the first to get closer if he deems to make some space by taking a little step back; if he wishes to turn you about, you must turn about in the same way. Go along with this game up until the moment, and as quickly as possible, you jump backwards or to the side and out of danger and break out of *corps-a-corps.* It is also one of the reasons why I advise one to know thoroughly, before he strikes, what lies behind and beside you on the duelling ground.

As soon as the *corps-a-corps* is over, place the épée in line ready to make a stop-thrust, or a parry and riposte or attack.

These are the principal special cases to consider.

Must one also add some observations on the subject of supposed "secret thrusts" which are sometimes spoken of?

When fencing was less advanced; when the game of parry, riposte and counter-riposte, its most astute play, was not well practiced certain unorthodox or disordered attacks were perhaps able to surprise even a trained adversary and find him unable to parry.

But today there is no such touch, however unorthodox it may be, which a trained fencer could not parry easily by ordinary means. And provided he takes up a proper guard, provided he is observant of the adversary's actions and holds himself ready to parry and riposte or attack, he has nothing to fear from he who tries an unorthodox attack from the school of secret thrusts of yore, and will even be able to injure him more grievously than after a regular attack.

Some of these famous touches are shown here:

Upon an attack pivot briskly to the side with a *demi-volte* and straighten the blade at the chest (*coup d'Angelo*).

Or else hold out the blade while dropping down by snapping the left leg backwards, or even making these presses from below while lowering oneself to the side, putting, as needed, the left hand on the ground!

All these bizarre touches are dangerous, especially for those who use them, because they encourage one to expose too much and lose their ability.

Difference in height- when there is an appreciable difference in height between two adversaries one finds a very interesting case where an épée fencer using his head will make up for any deficiencies in physical ability.

But what is a shorter fencer to do against a much taller fencer?

Because the fencer is short it is not to say that he must fashion an entirely new game from the taller fencer and that, for example, he must attack less. In reality he will have an equally varied game, perhaps even more varied. For attacks he uses them as much as parries and ripostes. Any fencer must know how to attack, in case his adversary does not attack.

Only a short fencer will use this particular method; he will gain the duelling ground by frequently accompanying his attacks with steps or little hops, or half-lunging, or even little longer to gain measure. Insist on little hops which, of course, must be done very carefully and without gaining more ground than if one used small steps.

As I have already shown a little step will be less rapid, less surprising to the adversary and done with less aplomb; what's more, while springing forward, as must be done, one will only risk of being touched on the advanced part.

We thus unite the two tempos of the step into one; which gains speed and authority and without giving away any advantage.

Regarding the method of executing the hop, one must observe well that it is combined with the attack. If he thrusts at the advanced part, disengage while springing, giving a one-two while springing &c.

Attacks to the body:

For the threatened croisé, spring while threatening the head (1) then give a croisé in seconde while stood still.

For a double-beat thrust direct in sixte, it will be best to begin from an engagement of quarte, then to demi-disengage to the arm, while springing, to then make a double-beat while stood still and immediately spring backwards.

Despite the great usefulness of these jumps, which the short fencer studies diligently, he must also practice, for variety, to step and gain measure.

They practice especially to gain measure after having half-lunged, to give counter-thrusts within proper distance.

Counter-riposte are particularly useful to them, as they allow them to approach progressively towards a taller adversary and those who stay far away.

To succeed they must either use jumps or gaining actions to the front, unless, of course, the adversary makes the advancing step or fully lunges, exposing him by his own means. To gain actions forward, the shorter fencer will practice gaining measure while attacking, sometimes returning to guard forward after half-lunging instead of returning backwards as is normal. While returning on guard forward, he must be ready to parry. In this way after having attacked while half-lunging, for example while disengaging to the arm, he returns to guard with his left foot forward instead of moving his right foot backwards, parrying the adversary's riposte while stood still, now being in proper distance, counter-riposte to the chest with convenience.

(1) If the adversary retreats after a threat, continue the attack to the arm

The shorter fencer will again find other techniques by using his head. Steps and counter-steps will be relatively easier for him than a taller fencer, he will make feints, as it were, with his legs, initially retreating as a first choice; after which, he will surprise the adversary with a step forward, while being ready to parry and riposte to the body. Sometimes, when one's adversary hesitates in the attack, he must, while stepping forward, beat or make changes of engagement that are a little large, to encourage the adversary to deceive them into a parry and riposte or counter-riposte.

A taller fencer must be sober in his actions. He seeks a little less to counter-riposte and hold his adversary at distance, in particular, avoiding letting him be gained in measure. He does not spring forward unless when his adversary retreats too often and too quickly. He does all this, of course, with great care, while avoiding becoming disorganised.

Observations on the game for left-handers

Due to lack of habit of fencing against left-handers, which is in fact quite a rarity, a right-hander will be surprised by the inversion of lines which result from this and therefore the right-hander will find that he will be "inside the épée" when in an engagement that is normally to the "outside" as he would be when fencing against another right-hander.

In other words, two right-handers together are generally engaged in the same line, whereas, when fencing a left-hander, a right-hander who takes, for example, an engagement of quarte will find his adversary engaged in sixte.

It is a good idea to spend some time fencing against left-handers if only so that one is not surprised by this inversion of lines.

As to a method for combatting left-handers the general principals of my method remain the same; but it is worthwhile to add the following observations.

The first concern of the right-hander, when fencing against a left-hander, must be to seek by all means possible to maintain an engagement of quarte. This is not only because there is a better cover in this line, but because it parries and ripostes more easily, and because his arm protects a good part of the chest in the case where the parry would be deceived. It is also because the left-hander will thus find himself in an unfavourable engagement for him, the engagement of sixte, which is less natural for him and where he has less freedom of movement and force than if he was in quarte.

Here is how to come on guard.

When it comes to attacks, as a general rule, from an engagement of quarte all the touches that one would make against a right-hander while from an engagement of sixte.

For attacks to the body, the double-beat direct thrust must be made from an engagement of quarte. The first beat in sixte, gently with a flying point; the second, more violent, will be a sort of expulsion in quarte finishing with a direct touch.

The croisé of seconde, recommended in this course of lessons, will be less practical against a left-hander than a right-hander, because one will find oneself less covered. But, against a left-hander, one could use a croisé finishing with a disengagement on an advanced part, without a lunge or with a half-lunge.

What's more, a threat in sixte followed by a bind in septime can be used against a left-hander because one can control an épée better in septime against a left-hander than against a right-hander. One must always be careful, after a bind, to not thrust at the body, but upon the advanced part.

As for choices of parries, those spoken of before will find their use for the larger part.

The parry of simple septime has greater authority against a left-hander than a right-hander. Alternate often, thus, in the low line, between this parry and that of seconde and it will be more useful to have a choice of parries in the low line as left-handers often thrust below.

The counter-sixte can also be used against left-handers, on condition that they end in a bind of septime or are done with a flying point in order to then make a violent beat in quarte and thrust to the body.

This sort of double parries are very useful for breaking the line and for preparing excellent ripostes or counter-ripostes.

In addition for the left-hander who holds his épée in the low line, it will be good to seek his blade with beats in septime or seconde in order to thrust immediately at the advanced part or the body if the beat was every vigorous. For variety sometimes make beats with the aim of having them deceived so that they prepare a riposte or counter-riposte.

The previous observations can be applied, as a general rule, to the game for left-hander against right-handers.

Specific Cases

Lessons on duelling for those who, on the eve of a duel, have never practiced fencing- What can be learned in several lessons- Advice to give, on the eve of a duel, to experienced foilists who have no game of the épée.

I have just exposed the game of the épée in its entirety in such that it can be learned by fencers who have previous experience with the foil or who have little time in front of them.

I shall examine several case studies where one is compelled to make singular choices in the game of the épée - at first let us take a most delicate one; one where a professor has in front of him someone who, on the eve of a duel, has never studied fencing.

What can he learn in this time with little preparation? For sure, one cannot create a complete fencer; some lessons on duelling are however of great use. They will give a novice combatant the means to have a suitable ability on the duelling ground, to embarrass his adversary, to receive a less severe injury if he is touched and sometimes even to touch a more skilled adversary who does not know the game of the épée.

In two or three lessons one can usefully practice getting on guard and see how to maintain proper measure; which is very important. What's more we must accustom him into having his point pointing forward while making some very simple attacks. Finally, practice controlling his steps, which is very important on the duelling ground. Let us see what must be taught on these in detail.

First he must be put on guard, making him take up a position in which he is least skewed, whatever that may be, because there is no the time to correct this position.

However one will recommend him to hold, as much as possible, his body upright and with aplomb so as to have greater grounding and freedom of action. If the body would be bent, the right arm will be skewed and the legs won't be able to move freely. Leaning forward would greatly risk being touched on the head.

Equally recommend him to hold his arm shortened for two reasons: first so that the extension of the arm is powerful while thrusting; it will, in effect, be more chambered in this position. What's more, one prevents the adversary from gaining the épée or, at least, it makes capturing it more difficult.

Then teach him to hold the point in a line as much as possible, placed well out in front, so as to directly threaten the advanced part which the adversary presents and that it can be reached as quickly as possible.

Once the guard has been taught, make him see at what measure he must put himself while on the duelling ground.

This distance is such that, when the épées are held well out in line, only the points are engaged and even then only just.

In effect, if one engages in combat too close he will give his adversary greater ease at gaining his blade and thrusting at his body. It is better to give him less blade while staying further away.

At the distance shown one is moreover close enough to reach, by means of a half-lunge, the adversary's arm. And one cannot be touched oneself, except upon the arm, even if the adversary lunges.

It is only for strong fencers to know when to approach and get closer.

The distance is thus taken, and noted with care.

It is very important that the inexperienced combatant tries maintain the distance which you have recommended to save getting a little too close through the combat.

While retreating and stepping especially, he must be certain that he does not break this distance too much. Furthermore, after you have shown him the guard and distance, one must practice controlling his steps.

In effect, as said elsewhere, a duel, as in combat, depends upon steps and counter-steps; but he must step or retreat in good time without exaggeration.

A novice combatant especially must not go forward without the greatest of care and making only little steps.

Practice controlling these forward steps and a variety of steps and jumps backwards so as to avoid an attack or a very quick riposte.

One can also remark to him at the same time that the step or jump back take the place of a parry as this is the most certain means of avoiding a touch.

What's more it is a little like the single parry which one can learn in one or a few lessons. It is thus doubly useful for a novice fencer to practice steps or jumps backward.

Thus prepared, put on guard, at the desired distance and practiced in stepping, retreating and jumping backward, it remains for him to learn some touches. Of course, these must be very simple. They consist of these:

Make beats in all lines and then punch the point straight out in front of you one, two or even three times, at the advanced part without lunging, or with a half-lunge, after which you will immediately spring back.

These beats have the aim of upsetting the adversary, and take his épée off-line; these sometimes have the advantage of serving as parries at the same time. Thus they are of very great use.

While making these beats, or launching a touch with the tip, it will be good to often make an appel with the foot so as to have greater aplomb, good grounding on the duelling ground and greater grace for throwing the touch.

I recommend also to immediately shorten the arm after each touch and to quickly return the épée point on line. He must launch and throw the touch as quickly as possible and with a brisk releasing action of the arm and then return immediately to guard.

An inexperienced combatant must do this every time in this game, either while stepping with small steps or while retreating.

If his adversary does not offer up his épée he must watch for an opportunity and upon every action punch straight out in front of him while always alternating between one, two or three thrusts with the point. Sometimes he should only throw out one thrust; sometimes he should redouble once or even twice. It is necessary to alternate thus to better deceive the adversary or at least to better embarrass his responses.

If the adversary still makes no actions while continuing to refuse his blade, threaten him to the face in order to bring his épée back on line and then thrust to the arm while punching and throwing a touch, as said before.

Such is the game to follow; it is unwise, in one or two lessons, to teach a more complicated game.

It is also important to not tire the pupil with this short preparation.

In this way, I teach him a game which exposes him least, due to the measure shown, and use beats which push aside the blade and unsettle the adversary. At the same time this game has the simplest tactics, which are the simplest thrusts and aims for the advanced part.

Beats and simple attacks are already liable to stop an adversary; the deed of punching with the point two or three times in a row without lunging, as learned in this lesson, contributes to interrupt the adversary who, threatened upon each action by these two or three thrusts with the point, finds himself forced, at risk and peril to himself do otherwise, to make him hesitate and be uncertain in his attacks, if he is not a strong épée fencer.

Other lessons may have advised him about the duel, notably, to hold his arm held out and outstretched.

No game is as dangerous as this one against a skilled adversary.

In fact, holding out the arm is to offer up the blade to the adversary as this provides a guide for gaining the épée, and it, at the same time as you advance, exposes too much of your arm and this will deprive oneself of all your means. In this position one cannot attack, nor parry, nor riposte.

By him clenching his arm strongly the adversary can push aside the blade by means of a double-beat finished with a sort of expulsion in sixte, or better control the blade while seizing the weak of the blade with the strong of his, then to immediately move it out and make a croisé of seconde.

A continuous tension of the arm is thus a great mistake; evermore it is very common that an inexperienced combatant who holds his arm outstretched in this way will, also, commonly tilt his head to the fore, while lying it along his arm, which exposes it to dangerous touches.

I have shown what can be taught in two or three lessons about the duel.

Another case: Someone who is about to duel but has never studied fencing but has a little time in front of him and can take eight or ten épée lessons before the duel. This is just enough to learn a more solid game and give him a greater chance. The guard will be taught better, and, especially, one will have the time to teach a few parries and ripostes.

Do not try to ingrain every parry and riposte but make him study the parries of counter-quarte and seconde in particular followed by ripostes and jumps backward.

As for attacks the professor will be content, most often, to teach thrusts to the advanced part. If, however, the pupil has the disposition, practice the two attacks to the body, as explained before; the threatened croisé and the double beat thrust direct in sixte.

If he comes along well in these dozen lessons one can advise him to try them on the duelling ground, but once or twice only and with care.

Now what to do with a skilled foilist who does not know the game of the épée but asks you to teach him on the eve of a duel?

If it is a foilist of mediocre ability, we are faced with something similar to the previous case.

But what if he is strong foilist? Épée in hand he should be capable making all the foil attacks while seeking the extremities and, what's more, the two attacks to the body which are the threatened croisé and the double-beat thrust direct in sixte. Sometimes even, he can thrust to the body after a single beat if he is especially vigorous.

What's more he can make a varied game of parries, but he must avoid using some like prime and quinte.

But, especially, he must take care to watch out for thrusts to the arm which foil won't have taught him to guard against, and to not risk disengagements or a one-two to the chest as he would perform them with foil.

Without this double precaution he will be exposed to singular surprises even against a less strong adversary.

The game of parry and riposte or counter-riposte will be, also, very simple for him.

In addition he must practice springing back after a touch to the body.

Observations upon the game for a strong épée fencer

1st Against a weak or mediocre adversary

2nd Against an adversary of equal skill

To wait, observe an adversary's faults and to do what is needed is above all, as I have said, the mark of a strong fencer.

As weak as his adversary may be, he does not dispense with his usual caution, observes every action attentively and does not make immediate attacks to the body.

On the other hand he makes many attacks on the half-lunge to encourage his adversary to attack, as he wishes, to then allow himself to parry and riposte in good measure.

He not only makes very simple parries but also slow ones if needed against an inexperienced fencer because they often make actions which are too large and, as a consequence, he must be wary of making his parries too quickly and missing the blade, then arriving too late.

All the same, as for ripostes, one must control his speed to match that of his adversary at least for compound ripostes.

For a *tac-au-tac* riposte, one can use all one's speed; but he must control his compound ripostes and allow the adversary time to make an action which expose shim. Without this precaution one risks a remise falling onto the blade.

In fact, an inexperienced fencer often makes remises.

To avoid these the strong épée fencer can use the croisé or double-beat which push aside the adversary's blade and allows a more certain path to the body.

Reprise attacks will often succeed for a strong fencer, as I have shown before, and will be a very practical technique against an inexperienced fencer who often stops after a fencing phrase while holding himself poorly on guard.

Now consider that the two épée fencers are of equal ability.

It is here that the game of the épée is revealed in all its splendour, in all its capacity, with its game of sober movements and very simple appearance which is, in reality, very varied.

Between two strong épée fencers the advantage will be to him who has the greater patience and "head" and to the one who can hold out for longer with composure and hold himself ready to profit from his adversary's smallest fault while avoiding any useless actions himself.

Certainly the adversaries cannot both hold themselves in expectation, in a very reserved fashion and prolonged manner; one of the two must begin the attack.

But he who does so must act with greatest of prudence, proceeding first with false attacks, feints and even occasionally with actions of the body. The latter must be done with be done with great caution.

The other combatant will be wary of these feints and false attacks. Sometimes, instead of responding, he must content himself with withdrawing the arm and refusing his blade; when he does respond, it will be with the intent of allowing a riposte or counter-riposte. Also he must take care as to only respond by a demi-action, so as to seek a counter-riposte for himself. At the same time both adversaries will study each other's favourite parries, and then deceive them. What's more, they should be wary of overlong fencing phrases which can lead to the unexpected and risk. To stop this, a strong épée fencer can break the line with a croisé or a double beat or, better, if he is poorly engaged and a little disorganised he then retreats with a jump backwards. On occasion, on the contrary, he will know not to let go, but continue to parry and riposte or counter-riposte - and if he seems to stop and return to guard, this will be to do a fast reprise of attack. Reprise attacks are a great technique for a strong épée fencer who sees that his adversary is a little disorganised by a fairly lively phrase. He must be wary himself, while holding himself on guard, and always be ready to parry even if a jump backwards has put him at fairly large measure.

Sabre duel

Sabre assaults, in the fencing salle, are less subject to conventions than those of the foil.

Everything is allowed in sabre; hits to the writs and the face as well as hits to the body.

But there remains some important differences between fencing in the salle and fencing in the duel, not only because of the practical conditions of the location, as I have explained for the épée, but also due to the danger that complicated cuts would offer on the duelling ground, which are usually used in the fencing salle.

Large movements from sabre fencing contributes to rendering them very dangerous. It results in stop-thrusts and double-hits. What's more double-hits are more frequent in sabre than in foil.

For these diverse reasons one must create a special duelling game for the sabre as with the épée.

In both cases the essential principal remains the same: by all means possible, bring the adversary to give himself, to offer himself within weapon reach and without offering oneself, this will be the general aim of a sabre fencer, being the same as for an épée fencer.

He seeks, above all, to be attacked frankly, so to parry and riposte, or counter-riposte to the body or the face after which, as in épée, he immediately jumps backwards.

On the matter of attacks, hardly does he ever make anything other than false attacks on the advanced part to make the adversary depart, to make him lunge and give them himself.

In addition, on the duelling ground, sabre fencers will avoid complicated feints made with the cutting edge, feints which are too exposing. What's more, they will use more the point of their weapon than in the assault in the salle. In the salle a sabre fencer hardly ever uses the point except for stop-thrusts. In fencing for the duel he must, on the contrary, when given the opportunity, use the point even as an attack and especially use it as a riposte.

75

When riposting with the cut one must take care to riposte in the same line as one parried. For example, they must take care to not commit the mistake of certain fencers who, after a parry of seconde or low prime, riposte with a cut to the shoulder or the face instead of riposting direct with a sabre cut to the flank or stomach. This leaves them exposed and leaves the adversary entirely free to remise.

It is much better to riposte direct. With exception, when there is a compound riposte, with a flying point, which is often very practical in sabre, the riposte which is finished with a wrist blow; aiming for the advanced target and made at long distance. The wrist blow exposes you much less than a blow to the body.

In riposte or attack the wrist blow is naturally recommended to sabre fencers in an affair against a stronger fellow.

I shall now concern us with several special cases, and initially those where the sabre fencer has in front him someone who only knows the use of the épée.

What must both adversaries do?

The sabre fencer must be wary of thrusts with the tip, the only ones which the adversary should be using. Sometimes he will stop him by wrist blows, sometimes by parry and riposte. Provoke as required these thrusts with feints with the sabre on the half lunge then parry and riposte either direct or with a flying point using a wrist blow.

What should the épée fencer, who has no knowledge of the sabre, do?

If he cannot, before the contest, take one or more lessons it is recommended that he solely uses the point of his weapon.

He shall place himself in the guard of tierce, the sabre guard; but in any case shall he make sabre blows, that's to say using cutting blows.

He will attack, as in épée, with disengages, direct attacks, the one-two, beats and aiming for the advanced part.

He will avoid certain thrusts, such as doubles, which are not very practical at sabre.

Often he will seek with a thrust to stop the adversary upon a preparation by making stop-thrusts to the arm, while the sabre fencer makes feints with cutting blows. He will also be wary that the sabre fencer is not actually provoking these thrusts so as to parry and riposte.

As for him, the épée fencer will launch sometimes his thrust as a false attack intended to make the adversary act, then try himself to parry and riposte or counter-riposte to the body but always with a thrust.

He will only make simple parries. The counters he uses in épée will not work in sabre, without exception. In effect they are more difficult to perform and less able to chase the blade.

In fact for simple parries the épée fencer will parry quarte, tierce or seconde. If he has several lessons in front of him I will exercise him in the use of the two other parries of sabre, high prime and low prime but it will be recommended to him to always riposte with a thrust.

By wanting to riposte with a cut, without habit, he will be too exposed; also he will make a bad cut, which must always be accompanied with a small sliding action of the sabre, so as to slice. If it is given with too much aplomb the sabre blow will not penetrate. This requires practice which the épée fencer does not have.

Suppose now a novice combatant, equally unable at the sabre as the épée. He is about to fight with the sabre against an adversary practiced in this weapon. What can he be taught in one or a few lessons?

He will be given exactly the same lesson as if he was going to fight with épée, except the difference that he will be shown the guard of tierce, the sabre guard.

He will be told to hold his arm back, point in line, body bent on the legs, left arm pressed upon the thigh.

Then he will be told to observe measure.

This done he will be recommended, upon all his adversaries actions, to launch one, two or three thrusts straight out in front of him to the advanced part and without lunging, or only with a half-lunge: after which he must leap backwards.

One will then perform beats in quarte and tierce before launching thrusts in the case where the adversary makes no preparation and no movements.

Beats of tierce and quarte, setting aside the adversary's blade, can make a passage of attack and, for the other part, can serve as parries. These are otherwise, along with jumps to the rear, the only parries which one can teach in one or a few lessons.

Set the inexperienced combatant to practice these thrusts, preceded or not with beats, while alternating between throwing one, two or three blows in succession, making this play while stepping or retreating.

Advice for the pistol duel

With good sight and attitude, a few months are enough to acquire good use of a pistol. From the particular point of view for the duel, especially a duel by command, a short period of preparation is sufficient.

The rules of shooting are few in number and very simple.

To be of good aplomb, good balance, the body upright, facing to the left, well profiled without hindrance, the right foot about thirty centimetres form the left foot, left hand upon the thigh, head turned toward the target.

Hold the grip of the pistol with the thumb and the last three fingers, the index placed on the trigger, and touching with the second knuckle. The first knuckle has less force to pull the trigger gradually. Holding otherwise, such as certain shooters do, with the middle finger on the trigger guard, holding the grip with the thumb, little finger and ring finger, this is not a habit to be advised, because it renders the action of the index finger on the trigger less delicate and less sensitive.

Before raising the pistol to eye height, one commonly holds the weapon lowered, arm straight and at an angle. One must guard against letting the barrel fall in the direction of your foot in case a jolt sets off the trigger.

All while holding the pistol lowered, get a good grip in the hand, make certain of the position of the body and see to it quickly that one is well placed to hit the target, that is that when the arm is raised it will bring the weapon up on a good line.

Instead of holding the pistol lowered before firing one can sometimes hold it pointing up, the arm bent at the height of the right breast. Sometimes, indeed, it happens that this position is adopted on the duelling ground. Certain known shooters prefer this position when practicing. In summary the question is of little importance.

Once the body is well placed and the pistol is properly held in the hand raise - or lower, as is the case - to eye-height and practice sighting by placing the weapon in such a way that the sightline passes through the notch of the rear-sight through the tip of the fore-sight and on to the target.

To have greater strength, acuity in the right eye, the eye with which one ordinarily sights, close the left eye and, furthermore, so as to benefit as quickly as possible in the direction of your sight, as soon that it is set, one must, while aiming, slowly attack the trigger, without jerking it, in such a way that, just as it begins to weaken, it pulls almost imperceptibly at the desired moment. In other words there should be no harsh pull, no roughness in the release. One must almost be surprised by release, which is gradually brought back, at the moment the weapon is well in line. Under these conditions your shot will not deviate.

One must become accustomed to sight quickly so as to be able, in a duel, to pre-empt the fire of your adversary. Practice shooting at all sorts of target preferably upon those known in public ranges as "the gentleman", otherwise a silhouette of a man of medium height and size.

One important remark to add is that, on the duelling ground, the pistols provided are often unknown to the adversaries, one must be wary of having a weapon with a set too light or too heavy; thus one must not pull the trigger until the barrel is raised to waist height on the adversary, for fear of being surprised by a very light trigger or a low shot but, furthermore, one must hold the grip more firmly than normal to impede a deviation in case the trigger is too strong.

Once familiar with sighted fire, one can practice firing on command, as is most used in duels.

On command, one must fire while the principal witness of the combat commands "Fire! One, two three!"

Before the command "Fire!" it is too soon to shoot; it is too late after the command "Three!"

The command "One, two, three" is ordinarily accompanied and sometimes replaced by three claps of the hand.

Here is the advice which must be given for a duel by command:

The commands are made very quickly upon the duelling

ground so one barely has time to aim at a given point.

If one wishes to do so, one risks firing too late, in other words after the command of "Three" has been given. Otherwise one exposes oneself to the first fire of the adversary, and, even admitting that it does not hit, the ignition alone of his weapon will cause, more or less often, disorder to the line of sight which one has begun taking.

It is much better, in summary, to not aim at a given point in a duel of command, unless one is well practiced and know how to sight very rapidly. Much better to seek only, in general, to shoot "down the line" as quickly as possible- "down the line" is to say at medium height and straight at the direction of the adversary.

To practice shooting in this way, one places oneself as stated for sighted shooting, but holding the grip more firmly. Indeed, so as to shoot quickly, one does not press the trigger gradually as when sight shooting and, as a consequence, it has the disadvantage of making a brisk blow to the finger upon release. By holding the pistol grip more firmly one can alleviate the deviation caused by the slight jerk which is common upon command, except among the very best shooters.

Ordinarily one holds the pistol low when waiting for the command.

Once well positioned and after having responded to the loader that you are ready, one must, on the command of "Fire!", rapidly raise the right arm in line, but do not begin pressing the trigger until the moment where the weapon is a little higher than waist height as explained previously.

Sometimes practice holding the weapon high while waiting for the command, as this position is sometimes adopted in a duel.

In this case do not squeeze the trigger until the moment that the weapon is at chest height, held straight and in line.

Advice for witnesses

Stages of an affair

Questions of the duel

The essay on the code of the duel, put together by the Count of Chateauvillars, based on the authority of its author's name, along with a number of signatures of men of the world who approved of it, as no other author would consider acquiring such an authority alone.

It is no less true that many able amateurs consider Chateauvillars partly out dated and subject to certain criticisms.

We have heard on this topic some many and interesting discussions in the fencing salles. It thus seems useful in exposing the principal ideas which are to be observed on the stages of an affair, on the roles of witnesses and the adversaries and on the diverse incidents which take place which will be addressed in "questions on the duel".

The duel is born of an offence or from an exchange of offences.

Due to an entirely natural rule of equality, the offended or the principal offended has the choice of weapons and, depending upon the degree of offence, has different rights as defined by Chateauvillars.

"The offended without grave insult chooses weapons which must be agreed by the aggressor.

"The offended with a grave insult or snub chooses the duel and the weapons.

"The offended with blows or injuries chooses the duel*, the weapons, the distance and can require that his adversary does not use weapons belonging to him, but he must, in such a case, also not use his own weapons either".

---

* What is meant by "Choose the duel"? This signifies, for example, that, for the pistol, one sets up an aimed duel instead of a duel of command or, if using the épée, one claims the right to wear a fencing or town glove.

The quality of offence thus gives different rights; it thus becomes more necessary to appreciate to the just validity of the nature of the offences and, in the case of an exchange of offences, knowing who has been principally offended. This often requires very delicate questions needing a very relative appreciation.

As is stated in Chateauvillars, a man who utters indecencies will not be recognised; these rules are to be undertaken for a serious injury not for impoliteness.

It is understood in general to say that, instead of seeking precise rules on the subject, one must allow a very great liberty in the judgement of the witnesses. It is for them to discuss and judge upon the circumstances of the affair. It is thus, in summary, a question of common sense more so than specific knowledge.

Even in the case where after an insult there has been a return by a hit or a punch, it is too often judged an absolute, as in Chateauvillars, that it is always he who receives the blow who is the offended. If the insult was very serious, and he responded to it, but not with a blow likely to injure but rather with a moral rather than physical offence, such as slapping him in the face with a glove, it is to be reckoned that a discussion by the witnesses is reasonable.

In the face of certain very serious insults, where an honourable man loses patience, it would become indecent that, grossly provoked by an adversary of little reputation, which could be better practiced in weapons, be forced to forfeit the choice of weapons because of a slap to the face with a glove or for having snubbed him.

Witnesses are advised to take even greater liberties on the questions of age, the vigour or infirmities of both adversaries, on the question of knowing if, in certain cases, one adversary can be replaced by another if, for example, a son may replace his father who is too feeble or aged to respond to an offence and to take his place, thus benefitting from the rights of the offended.

The call for witnesses is often preceded, when the adversaries know of each other a little, by an exchange of cards. In this case, the offended, or whoever is considered to be such, gives his card and demands that of the offender. Then each goes off in search of two witnesses.

If the adversaries are close friends, it is often advisable that the offended or principal offended, before calling for witnesses, attempts an official approach from a mutual friend, as long as the offence is not too serious.

The mutual friend will be charged with asking in an amicable way for explanations or a retraction. Taking the title of advisor and attempting to discuss the matter with the offender- which a witness must never do- he will obtain an arrangement much more easily safeguarding the dignity of both parties. If this official step is not successful, the offended then seeks two witnesses, but he will be grateful for having attempted reconciliation imposed by old friendship.

As the offended seeks out two witnesses, the adversary must, without delay, request two friends to be ready at his disposal.

Witnesses must be men of obvious perfect honour. One must choose those with a steady spirit, not easily broken. One of the two, at least, must be well skilled in weapons to then fulfil the requirements of the duelling ground. In the case of an épée duel this mission is often difficult.

As is shown in Chateauvillars, for reasons easy to understand, a father, brother, son or a close-relative cannot be a witness to his own parent or against his own parent.

For the same reason one cannot choose witnesses from among the people offended by a collective insult and all demanding reparation, or who took part in the collective insult motivating the duel.

The same goes for all people known to have violated the rules and conditions of the duel or who have authorised this violation that they cannot be chosen as witnesses.

As to how to understand the role of witnesses, which is important, there are two fairly different systems which have formed on the subject of the intent of their powers.

Following a system developed by well known amateurs, the witnesses, once chosen and made aware of the affair, become masters of the situation, arranging the affair or deciding the duel as they wish and under the conditions they wish. Their client enters no discussion with them and submits to them entirely. The same, when directing the combat, they are attributed discretionary powers.

This system is excellent, if subscribed to, if one always has competent witnesses with authority. But these are very rare.

More often the witnesses ignore the object of their mission, or if they have some idea about it, are barely capable of performing it in all cases. One knows, furthermore, of all the epigrams launched against witnesses started by a certain Alphonse Karr,

> "It is not the épée, nor the pistols which kill: it's the witnesses."

Not only on the duelling ground do they prove to be inexperienced; even at the start of their mission very few know how to acquit themselves in a regular fashion and safeguard the rights of their client. They let themselves be dominated by more experienced, more devious witnesses, and often influenced by those who are known names foremost in fencing, afraid to overrule them, hesitant to make objections, ending up allowing them to be persuaded that their client is wrong and that he must accept all sorts of shortcomings, such as accepting this or that unfavourable condition, even when right is on their side.

For these diverse reasons many amateurs prefer to hold to the Chateauvillars method, which does not give discretionary powers to the witnesses and gives a little greater liberty to the adversaries in their conduct. This is my advice.

Each adversary must try to control and discuss with both his witnesses the plan to be followed.

He must be frank and complete about the true cause of the affair, towards his real and apparent motives and upon the terms that he will accept by arrangement, or better, in the case of combat, upon the conditions which he thinks he will have the right to refuse or accept.

One can furthermore consult a competent and reputable fellow on the matter. If the frank and complete explanations given to the chosen witnesses, with exception maybe, certain private details, such as the name of a woman for example, if these explanations are not entirely at their convenience, for one reason or another, they think that they should not be involved in the affair, or they do not agree with their friend upon the conditions on which the difference will be ended, they will refuse themselves as witnesses and they will retire without betraying the secret of the affair which their friend desired to confide in them.

Conversely, one must be able to thank them, even when rejected, for avoiding all wrinkles in their self-esteem and even better that the separation took place sooner rather than later, better that, from the start, that there is no bad intent or misunderstanding.

This freedom of action does not exclude the confidence of their client in their friendship, but the client can be overruled by more expert witnesses.

In default of greater experience, they can have greater energy for refusing unfavourable conditions, since he is the one involved in the cause of the matter, and it is he who will fight.

But, as it is objected, he lacks the composure, the necessary calm precisely because he is the cause.

Let us respond that, in general, one must suppose of people that the prospect of a duel will not trouble them to this degree.

If the contrary is the case, the witnesses will seek to intervene more greatly, influencing more than usual with their advice on the stages of the affair.

In all cases, moreover, the role of the witness stays very important and implies great strength of responsibility at the start of the affair, and often on the duelling ground.

Once the two witnesses are decided they go to the home of the adversary and they hand over their cards with the note, "On behalf of Mr X."

If the adversary is not found at home the witnesses leave their cards while stating the exact hour that they will meet or indicating the meeting place.

If upon their second visit the adversary is once again absent they will warn in writing that if they haven't received from him, within twenty four hours, a letter fixing the meeting place the witnesses will consider it a refusal.

The delay for sending out witnesses is ordinarily twenty four hours. The same is given for a response. But, depending upon circumstances, such as unpreventable circumstances, the witness will appreciate that they are not to prolong any delays in the proceedings.

When the witnesses of the offended meet the adversary, they will explain to him in a very polite manner the point of their visit which is to obtain reparation in the form of a retraction, an excuse or an encounter: when with the adversary they must make a point of not discussing the facts which motivate the duel as it is later, with the adversary's witnesses, that this will be discussed.

Again they must see that the adversary is not indulged in making recriminations against the conduct of their client.

The adversary must, furthermore, understand that this is a matter of tact and that he has received perfect courtesy from the witnesses toward their adversary and that, in return, he must say nothing against them.

The witnesses must retire if the adversary persists, in spite of their observations, in discussing the facts and put aside any verbal processes.

The adversary must, without detour, speak the course of action he will take.

This course of action must be, in general, that he will recruit witnesses.

It is assumed, that it is always better to engage witnesses as a response to a visitation from witnesses, even when the quarrel is only slightly serious and judged that there is no reason to fight. Indeed, in the case of a refusal of witnesses, the opposing witnesses will draw up a missive stating this refusal and this commonly has a poor outcome, especially if the missive is made public.

What's more an amicable arrangement is made with more dignity between four witnesses. The lone adversary who arranges with the opposing witnesses is set up sometimes to cede to their pressure.

The accused will give his witnesses addresses to the witnesses of the opposition. They will then request a meeting with the named witnesses.

Convene a meeting as convenient as is for all.

The two adversaries must never engage in the discussion between the four witnesses and especially they should never enter discussions with each other.

The four witnesses once gathered examine at first the real or apparent motives behind the affair. They discuss the cause, examining whether there is any bad intent or misunderstanding, if it is possible to arrange and end the affair, which they must try to do as much as possible. If not the case, they judge the gravity of the quarrel and whether the wrongs are from one or other of the adversaries or whether the two are both at fault.

After these discussions the witnesses, except those particular experts to which their client has wholly relied upon, will return to him to pass on the explanations of the opposing witnesses and thus to know what outcome they must decide to take and under what conditions. Everyone knows that if they do not agree with their client they can excuse themselves from their duty and their client can then appoint a new witness.

Let us look at what different outcomes the witnesses, with the client's approval, can take with the opposing witnesses.

Is it understood that there is insufficient argument for an affair?

Then the four witnesses make up a record of their discussion, sign and date the missive, which has been agreed upon by all beforehand, and send it to all parties concerned.

If, on the contrary, there is sufficient offence it must result in a retraction or a meeting.

As for apologies, the form the apology takes depends upon the gravity of the offence; if it was very serious and in public the offended party can and must seek an apology, and a public apology at that. The reparation must be in accordance with the offence.

If a duel is arranged one must not, once at the duelling ground, accept an excuse.

The role of the adversary and the witnesses would be held in ridicule if it were to get that far without a fight.

If those who wish to make their excuses upon the duelling ground persist in refusing to fight it must be recorded in a missive.

One should not content oneself with a simple retraction upon the duelling ground.

However, it admitted that a retraction made in proper time is often an acceptable form of arrangement and that, depending upon the circumstances, it is no stain on the dignity of he who concedes to it, especially if the adversary makes, off his own bat, certain concessions.

The witnesses must write, in a missive, the retraction or the excuses made and declare if they seem reasonable, and if they are to be made public or not.

Once the offender has made reparation of this type and all is judged to be sufficient there is no more reason to duel. For there to be a duel there must be another quarrel, a new affair; it is those who wish to continue who become the aggressor and, after common opinion, there is not any need to resort to choose new weapons again, despite the contrary advice of Chateauvillars.

Now I come to the case where a quarrel is deemed sufficient to justify an encounter from which neither of the adversaries can excuse themselves nor retract.

Sometimes a question is posed; that of a jury of honour. One of the adversaries declares that he is ready to fight; but, having doubts about the honour of his antagonist, he calls a jury of honour which must decide if he is worthy of fighting.

An allegation of this sort is clearly very grave and an attack which must not be composed without serious and real evidence against he who is the subject.

Those who convene a jury of honour are often criticised for seeking to prevaricate in order not to fight, or trying to use delaying tactics.

It is considered better in general not to pose this previous question. If you have doubts on the honour of your adversary ready your witnesses to make a rapid enquiry on your account, with no question of a jury of honour. If this enquiry is unfavourable and the remainder of your adversaries witnesses are themselves the subject of caution you may refuse the duel. But if he has reputable, honourable witnesses he is covered by his witnesses and to refuse the duel on your part will be interpreted badly.

Now that this question is ruled out, let us see what should be done when an encounter is accepted in principle by both parties. It is now a matter of settling it.

The witnesses of each adversary will naturally try to enforce his own conditions. It can happen that they disagree upon the question of who is the principal offended or upon the extent of this qualification for the right to decide the nature of weapons and the duel.

In such a case, always after having referred to their clients, the witnesses will draw by lot the type of weapons or defer to arbiters or a jury of honour.

Once the conditions of the combat are ruled the witnesses must relate them in a missive.

This missive before the duel is very important and must be very detailed even more so than normal. One very often only indicates what weapon is chosen, if a fencing glove is permitted and if the combat will be stopped after the first injury. This is not sufficient. There must be no misunderstanding. It must be that the adversaries and witnesses must know well under what conditions they are to fight.

Certainly one should not establish complicated conventions which will trip up inexperienced combatants and be particularly worthy of interest. But it must be made certain that the adversaries and witnesses know what's what on the important questions, such as knowing whether they can separate them or not in the case of a *corps-a-corps,* if the use of the left hand is forbidden, if there will be rests and if they can retake the field.

Show the conditions of combat in the missive clearly in advance so that the adversaries can read it before the combat, this is an essential precaution so that the combat will go ahead correctly and without unfair surprises.

With regard to the way in which the above matters need to be addressed, in general, that everything in a duel is in agreement.

One can stipulate a duel with masks and plastrons; a duel to first blood or going until the physical impossibility of continuing; one can stipulate that the adversaries are not separated in the case of a *corps-a-corps* without exception. In pistol one can determine such-and-such a distance, or such-and-such number of shots. One can make, in summary, all sorts of conventions. It is up to the adversaries to know how they wish to fight and to agree on the subject with their witnesses.

Only the "exceptional" conditions of combat outside of a "legal" duel are to be refused by the offended, as explained in Chateauvillars.

For their part, the witnesses must in general not arrange exceptional conditions of combat.

Here are, concerning the principal questions as ruled on in the missive before the duel, the uses that are generally allowed.

Nature of weapons

There are three sorts of weapons deemed legal; the épée, the pistol and the sabre.

Any other weapon is by mutual agreement. One can arrange, for example, that one takes up the foil but the offended can refuse this.

As for the sabre, even though it as a legal weapon, Chateauvillars adds:

> "The sabre can be refused by an aggressor if he is an officer in retirement and does not deem it proper to make use of it. It can always be refused by a civilian."

I have often seen this capability given to the offender to refuse the sabre criticised. Why this difference between the sabre and the épée? Is it because one is more practiced in the fencing salle? All the more reason as, in my opinion, it is because this lack of practice will often contribute to equalising the chances.

Use of the town glove and the salle glove

Every combatant always has the right to wear a town glove. Furthermore one can agree that both combatants can have a salle glove.

But the difficulty is to know if the offended can impose on the offended the use of a salle glove which prevents in part hits to the forearm.

As a general rule it is agreed that one does not protect the forearm or any other part of the body on the duelling ground and as a consequence the offended must not be allowed to impose a salle glove upon the offender.

It is a question of convention upon which advice is much divided.

Resting during combat- reprises

Following general opinion one must not stipulate that it will be defended to take a break to catch one's breath during combat.

Certain object, it is true, that one fights as much with his physical energy and with his lungs as with the science he has in arms.

It would be unjust, however, when an adversary is not a regular in the fencing salle, has not trained and perhaps lacking in breath, is not given the possibility to take a breath from time to time. In such case he could be almost disarmed and it would be unjust to not interrupt the combat.

Of course there must not be an abuse of these interruptions and it is for the doctor to see if there is bias, without sufficient reason, to demand a break. As for the manner of how to ask for a break, I will cover it while talking about what is to happen during the duel.

The reprise of combat must be made as quickly as possible.

One can agree with others that the break will take place at fixed intervals of time, every five minutes, for example, or else upon the request of a combatant, with the indicated restrictions.

Means for retaking the field in the case of becoming cornered

What is the best course of action in the case where one of the adversaries comes cornered?

First note the chosen duelling ground must have enough space to allow sufficient steps and counter-steps; each adversary must have on average twenty-five to thirty metres of space behind him at the start of the combat.

In default of this space, it becomes just to agree that the cornered combatant is able to retake the field, one, two or even three times.

Even if one is disposed to have a very large space the witnesses must allow a cornered combatant to retake the field when this cornering happens accidentally and is unforeseen- not due to the skilful step of the adversary who, in the latter case, would be a legitimate use of the duelling ground.

Corps-a-corps

Corps-a-corps brings too often, almost forcefully, misconduct. It degenerates easily into wrestling with a weapon in hand, where one fences as one can, no matter how, and where it is very difficult, especially with inexperienced combatants, to not make instinctively serious mistakes, resulting, for example, the use of the left hand. Trained fencers themselves cannot guarantee, when *corps-a-corps,* that they will never diverge from the rules of fencing.

In any case, combatants, trained or not, are trained to continue combat, when *corps-a-corps,* even after having touched their adversary.

It happens often that there is not even a doubt that the adversary is wounded.

Despite these reasons *corps-a-corps* must not be proscribed, a priori. It is a serious incident in the duel; where the combatants, while upon the duelling ground, must accept the eventuality of incidents of this type.

It is also very difficult to easily separate both adversaries in a case of *corps-a-corps;* the witnesses must thus not consent to a ban on *corps-a-corps,* a ban that they cannot even be sure they have the power to substantially enforce.

However, though it is not a convention in the duel, the witnesses, in agreement with the adversaries, are clearly free to agree to stop *corps-a-corps.*

Of course if they have been included in the missive the witnesses must, if *corps-a-corps* constitutes a misdemeanour then try, at any cost, to stop. There is *force majeure.* It will be shown in the following section what means must be used.

Use of the left hand for parrying or right hand in the case of left-handers

The question is of course to know if one can set aside the opposing épée with this hand. Concerning seizing it; there is no discussion to be had, it is absolutely inadmissible.

The parry which consists of setting aside the blade with the left hand should not be advised; it constitutes a disadvantage for he who uses it because it can lead to being exposed and at the same time impeding the action of his right arm.

It is why it has been banned from use in our fencing salles where it had been taught for a long time (see Gomard).

In a duel, the opposition of the left hand has the inconvenience for he who sets aside the blade is tempted to grab it at the same time. This circumstance must be avoided, especially so as it will be often difficult for the witnesses to perceive if the blade was seized or simply set aside.

For these reasons, in summary, it is better to proscribe the use of the left hand, and I do not advise anybody, whether an experienced fencer or not, to claim the right to parry with the left hand on the duelling ground.

However, since everything in a duel is done by convention, one can admit this parry in the missive. It must be understood; in the case of silence in the missive on the subject it must be that the left hand is implicitly proscribed.

In addition, in the case where it is allowed, it will be useful to use gloves furnished in such a way that the left hand cannot be closed or the épée seized.

As for tying back the left arm, as has been proposed, I know not of amateurs who would consent to fight under these conditions.

These are the principal conventions to establish for the épée duel.

All of the conventions which have been demonstrated are also applicable to the sabre duel. One sometimes adds to the sabre this special convention that hits with the point are forbidden. In this case one makes use of sabres with a rounded tip.

I do not advise the adoption of this exceptional condition, which can in every case be refused even by the offender. I advise that the use of the point is, as I have said, very practical in a sabre duel.

As for the special conventions for the pistol duel, I will speak of them elsewhere.

Once the conditions for combat have been well established, the witnesses clearly demonstrate them in the missive which is communicated between the adversaries.

The witnesses must follow up by seeking a duelling ground and weapons on the eve of the duel.

Without these precautions one risks most unnecessary delays for everyone, some minutes before the combat and in front of the adversaries. It is better in every way that the duelling ground has been scouted out the evening before and the weapons well chosen, adversaries drawing and crossing swords within five minutes of arriving at the meeting place.

One must choose level ground, fairly large and especially fairly long. It is good, as I have said, that the adversaries have twenty-five or thirty metres behind them. It must also be free as possible of pebbles, sand, grass and obstacles which will impede his steps or be slippery. Finally, in the case of sun, one must seek out a shady spot.

Equally, on the eve of the duel, the épées must have been seen by the witnesses.

They must be easy in hand, well balanced, have hilts of regular proportions, and not too heavy. For length adopt that of a no.5 foil or thereabouts.

They must not be edged nor burred.

It is of no consequence whether they have been used before, provided they only have slight abrasions.

At the end of one minute of combat a new épée becomes abraded anyway.

One must also occupy oneself with choosing a director of combat on the eve.

This direction must be entrusted to the witness with the most experience, the most notable, or in the case of a contest on the matter, of the greatest age.

If two opposing witnesses are both of known competence one can then admit both of them to direct the entire combat.

If there is only a single director of combat it will be natural that there will be a complete impartiality between his client and his adversary.

Besides, without having the same title, the other witnesses will be there to direct the task of the director to support or impede him as they see fit. They should not hold a passive role, where they would appear to be disinterested in the combat.

Let me add that the interventions of the director of combat in civil duels must not be compared to those of a master of arms in military duels.

The latter has for a task not only to impede all incorrect incidents but also to parry dangerous attacks. In civil duels on the contrary, the director of combat must only interpose himself to prevent a foul blow and stop the duel in the case of incorrectness. But if the adversaries observe the rules and the conventions, he will not, under no pretext, intervene by parrying a dangerous blow.

It is not necessary to show in the missive who will be the director of combat. It is even better to do this to avoid crushing any self-esteem.

Another question of rules on the eve of a duel is to seek out doctors.

In general rule each adversary must bring a doctor. This is most correct and moreover one must predict the circumstance where the adversaries are both injured.

On the duelling ground

Once the adversaries and witnesses arrive on the duelling ground, as previewed the evening before, the director of combat takes in hand the management of the affair.

He first draws lots to see where to place the two adversaries. There must be equal advantage as much as is possible.

Both pairs of épées which have been brought along are equally drawn by lot.

This done, show each adversary to his place. Both must look in front and around themselves to better know the nature of the duelling ground and the obstacles where they may become trapped.

Then they are told to remove anything that could parry an épée hit. Make them unbutton their collar, allowing them to keep anything that is not an obstacle to épée points, such as flannel vests or shirts.

It is of little importance whether the shirt is starched or not; it is often recommended to combatants to make sure it is well-starched because it can sometimes make the épée point slide off. But it is better to have a shirt starched normally, or even un-starched so as to not impede your movements.

Everything which can parry an épée blow must be removed; belts and braces. One must declare if one has a bandage, and in each case, this is a matter of judgement for the witnesses.

They must visit each adversary patting them down quickly to assure themselves that his shirt has nothing that protects him in an underhand way.

All of these preliminaries must be made quickly but without negligence.

Once these precautions are taken and both adversaries are ready for combat the director of combat paces them seven or eight paces, or even a little further, apart facing each other.

He places himself a little to the side, having near to him the witness of his client's adversary. Opposite him, on the other side of the adversaries, must be placed the other two witnesses. It is under these conditions that one will be able to follow the duel and observe it.

The director of combat goes to each adversary and gives him an épée. He reminds them that they must not start the combat before he has said "Go, sirs!" and, what's more, once the épées are crossed they must stop upon the command of

"Halt!" He also reminds them that they must not speak during the combat, except to ask for a rest if that has been agreed.

After which, ordinarily, he tells them to hold out their arms, take up the very end of both épées, then approach each other until tip to tip, though a small distance from each other, and after having observed if both adversaries are ready to come on guard he says, "Go, sirs!" and lets go the épées.

But it is better, on my advice, thus to avoid a surprise, to place the adversaries out of measure before saying "Go, sirs!"

The combat begins. At the signal of "Go, sirs!" each adversary will fall backwards into guard, or even retreat a pace to avoid a surprise if one has not taken the precaution shown.

During the duel the director and witnesses, placed as told, stay five or six places from the combatants. They will approach at need when it seems their intervention has become necessary.

In what cases and how must one intervene?

They intervene not only in the case of injury but in the case of;

1ly-disarms, 2ly- épée breakages, 3ly-falls, 4ly- accidental cornering, 5ly-a rest is granted, 6ly- *corps-a-corps;* if it has been agreed that they will be separated in such a case, 7ly- when a someone has committed a foul blow.

Before examining these diverse cases we shall see what manner of intervention will be made.

The adversaries are without doubt forewarned that on the command of "Halt!" that they must stop.

But this command is not sufficient. In the heat of battle one combatant may continue even though his adversary has stopped.

It is better that the command "Halt!" is supported by an effective intervention by the director of combat alone or aided by a witness.

It is often the difficult part of their role and in particular when there is *corps-a-corps.*

Besides the dangers that one can run into when separating épées in spirited *corps-a-corps,* there is a fear, if one takes one slightly awkwardly, of not stopping one of the adversaries. What a responsibility for the witness if the adversary who has not stopped thus gives a blow to his adversary, injuring or killing him!

It is clear for this part of his task, that a witness particularly must have presence, a real competence in weapons and know when to apply it positively and with presence of mind.

If at the side of each adversary is found an experienced witness, these two witnesses must understand and undertake to stop each of the combatants in the frequent case where he must, whatever the cost, try to stop them, that is to say when a foul has been committed.

Each one will seize the arm of one of the combatants, or remove his épée with a cane or simply with a hand.

If there is only one expert witness, having been charged solely in directing the combat, he must try various methods to separate both adversaries: sometimes he will try to lift up the épées with the aid of a cane; sometimes he will seize the arm of each adversary or, from one side oppose with his left arm, and the other seize the arm or épée of one of the combatants with his right hand.

Let us now examine each of these incidents which can come about during combat and provoke an intervention.

Disarms

In the case of a disarm, the director of combat and, if required, the other witnesses, must intervene to stop the combat, returning the épée to the disarmed adversary and returning him to his place in front of his adversary.

What to do if a combatant injures his unarmed adversary? Judgement must be used.

If the blow immediately followed the disarm, if it was given with tac au tac, after a parry or beat, he who has injured was perfectly within his rights and the blow would have landed anyway. On the contrary, if there was a marked interval between disarm and injury: if he who disarmed noticed and had time to stop himself he commits nothing less than murder or attempted murder.

Besides the director of combat incurs a grave liability if he does not prevent an injury thus made in the case of a disarm except, I repeat, when the blow is given in *tac au tac*.

This is the reason why the director of combat must have a real competence at arms.

Épée breakages

Once more the witnesses must intervene and stop the combat.

All the same the adversaries must stop themselves once they have observed the incident. One may recommence the combat with another pair of épées.

Falls

The same is necessary for the witnesses to intervene. The adversary of he who has fallen must equally stop himself.

Cornered

If it is agreed that a cornered combatant may retake the field, stop the combat *at the very moment* that the he begins to be cornered; then one can retake the field and recommence the combat.

On the contrary, if the adversaries have a very great deal of free space behind them and one of the two abuses this to retreat indefinitely the witnesses must stop the combat to make their observations. They can even place a barrier of some sort or define a boundary to stop this type of flight.

Of course, this is not previewed in the missive. Let us add that even if one is not always permitted to retake the field, one must at the least warn the combatant upon the point of being cornered, so that he is not surprised too briskly by an object near to which he can hurt himself. What's more, it is correct for him to become familiar with the duelling ground before coming to guard.

Pauses and restarting the combat

The director of combat stops both adversaries and makes them take a break at each interval for a fixed period as in the missive or, better, when one of the combatants is visibly fatigued. Besides one can himself ask; he can, for example, make one or two steps backwards, lower his épée and say "I demand a break".

The break must last one or two minutes at most; doctors may extend this period; also one must not accept it when a combatant makes an abuse of these demands.

The rest period having elapsed, the director of combat calls the adversaries into his presence, in the same way as at the beginning.

Corps a corps

I have already demonstrated a great part on the concerns of *corps-a-corps*. In the case of absence in the missive, the combatants have every liberty to infight, unless it brings about a foul. A foul move forces an intervention from the director of combat and, if required, the other witnesses.

Violations of the rules and conventions of the duel

These violations can be of a very different nature and gravity.

In certain cases, the witnesses must stop the combat immediately and consult the missive.

Let us quickly see the various fouls which can be brought about.

During the combat it is allowed to jump to the side, to make turning movements to gain the duelling ground or favourable light which are legitimate ways of winning.

It is allowed to retreat fairly far and for a fairly long time; often, besides, this will be a type of tactic intended to give the adversary an excess of confidence. While retreating one must, of course, sustain sufficiently the combat and not be making some sort of flight. This is up to the witnesses to appreciate. I have said before, furthermore, that if an adversary leaves the combat too much they can revert to this, then, if he continues, interpose an obstacle of some kind or define a boundary to stop his flight.

They will warn him when he gets too close to this obstacle or boundary. If he escapes anew, or goes beyond or stays alongside for a fixed period, the witnesses must definitively stop the combat and consult the missive.

If the adversaries talk under arms the director of combat must prevent it, stopping, if required, the combat to give a warning. In the case of recurrence, despite his warnings, he will deliberate with the other witnesses if he should or should not stop the duel.

This last solution is imposed when a combatant commits a grave refusal to obey the witnesses or when he wants to oppose their legitimate intervention.

It will be the same if a combatant insults his adversary or one of the witnesses for a stronger reason if he wants to indulge his insult.

He can thus cut short the affair and address the missive.

Injury

The director of combat and other witnesses must observe the movements of the épées in such a way as to perceive immediately that a blow has landed.

Without waiting for blood to flow, for this will be too long, he must stop the combat as soon as a épée-blow touches the shirt or trousers, thus to check whether it has penetrated.

The combatants can take the lead to acknowledge an injury.

Doctors approach, examine the wound or wounds received by a combatant or by both. When one is injured a witness goes near to his adversary and, if required, recommends that he stays some paces away and maintains his silence.

The wound sometimes leads to the end of the combat, sometimes a simple interruption.

If the injury is light and does not give too much disadvantage to the injured the combat can recommence, upon the advice of the doctors and if the conventions of the missive are not against it.

In general, as I have said, the missive maintain that one fights until it is impossible to continue. The doctors decide this impossibility; adversaries and witnesses must insist to those near them that they do not stop the combat on the behalf of a minor wound.

After the duel

Once the duel has finished the witnesses must forthwith make a summary in the missive or as soon as possible.

This missive must be very brief, quickly mentioning the day, hour, place of combat, number of reprises, the result and the principal cause which brought it about.

It must not contain an observation on the conduct of the combatants but simply state the facts. Any mention that honour was satisfied is judged not useful.

The missive must be signed by the four witnesses.

But it sometimes comes about that they cannot agree and that the two witnesses of each adversary make their own missive. This is always their right, but in the case where two witnesses write against the adversary of their client a minute seeking to impeach his honour, the adversary witnesses must appreciate that they must protest against certain allegations, and by which means and in what fashion. Their protestations will impeach only their client; but they must take the lead, and absolutely cover him.

Once the missive is signed by common accord by the four witnesses, as is frequently the case, not one of them can henceforth bring about any changes to the information in the missive by himself alone and under any pretext.

Conventions of the pistol duel

All that has been said on the role of the witness for an épée duel is naturally applicable to the pistol duel.

The nature of establishing the conventions differs only in two cases.

There are several forms of pistol duel: the most used that of the duel on command.

Recall that in this duel the witness who is director of combat, once the adversaries are in place and have arms in hand, asks of them "Are you ready?" and upon their affirmative response commands "Fire! One, two, three", while striking with his hand. Under penalty of committing a form of murder, or attempted murder, the adversaries must not shoot before the command of "Fire!" nor after "Three".

The orders are normally pronounced fairly quickly; the interval must be ruled upon in advance by the witnesses.

The usual distance, for the duel of command, is twenty paces. The minimum is fifteen paces. The witnesses must hesitate to consent to less than twenty paces.

Ordinarily one agrees that the adversaries discharge two or four balls.

The duel with aiming, employed very rarely, is ruled by a different method. Of course, the adversaries must not aim for too long. There would be a sort of barbarity to letting a combatant who shrugged off the fire of his adversary and who furthermore no longer had any fear, holding his fire indefinitely. If however the first aimed for a long time before firing it would not be too much pressing for the other.

Furthermore Chateauvillars proposed to fix a one minute interval during which both adversaries must aim and fire after a signal.

Both must be allowed to act at the same time; at least, that would appear preferable. Chateauvillars allows successive fire in a duel. The combatants fire in this case one after the other, either a draw decides who gets to fire first or that the offender has decided to cede to the offended. But one reckons that a convention of this type is not advised and perhaps in every case can be refused even by the offender. In effect it is only a true combat if both adversaries fire upon each other at the same time.

In addition in the case of successive fire, after Chateauvillars, the combatant who fires second has a minute to riposte from the moment where his adversary has given fire, and even two minutes if he has been injured.

One can agree that the aimed duel will be done stood still or walking. For example, the adversaries are placed at thirty paces, with the ability to each advance by five paces.

This double walk-up succeeds in giving the duel an appearance of true combat.

One typically agrees, as for the command, that the adversaries discharge two or four balls. As for distance, the aimed duel is ordinarily from twenty-five paces.

I shall not speak of other conventions sometimes allowed, which are exceptional, complicated and useless in a pistol duel. One must clearly abstain from conventions such as those where a single pistol is loaded and the weapons allocated by lot. This is no longer combat.

Once the conditions of the duel are ruled and the missive finished the witnesses are set on the direction of combat. This direction is to be, as with a duel with épées, entrusted to the most experienced of the witnesses, the most distinguished or eldest; he must have an absolute impartiality between the two adversaries, an impartiality which the other witnesses must control.

Also on the eve of the duel, the witnesses must occupy themselves with the choice of arms and duelling ground.

In general the weapons must be unfamiliar to both combatants.

They must be a matched pair. The sight must be fixed. By exception, after Chateauvillars, it is allowed that each combatant will serve himself with a weapon belonging to him but on the condition that the pistols are no different in length by more than three centimetres and they are of the same calibre.

Once the pistols are chosen the witnesses place them in a sealed case which will only be opened on the duelling ground.

For greater security, and a matter of great importance as the accuracy of the shot depends upon the loading, one must not load the weapons until the last moment, upon the duelling ground, and done by a designated witness, chosen by lot or by previous agreement, who must load the weapons in the presence of the other witnesses. He will take care to first fire the weapons, loaded from a cartridge with a blank charge, to clear the barrels.

On the eve of the combat one of the two witnesses will set out on a quest for a duelling ground. They must choose the sort of place with no physical objects, no trees, no bushes nor wall which will serve to direct the shot of one adversary over the other.

Once on the duelling ground choose places by lot, with equal advantage however possible, and allocated in such a way that neither adversary is facing into the sun or the wind. The combatants may remove or fasten their overcoats at their own volition. They typically retain their hair. They are always allowed to raise the collar of their coat to conceal the reference point which is formed by the white collar of their shirt- a very useful aiming point against the sombre fabric.

The witnesses quickly visit the adversaries, who have removed every object which can stop a ball, their wallet, their watch, their coin-purse and even coins.

After which the director of combat positions both adversaries and hands them the primed weapons (1).

He then retires immediately to the side with the other witnesses, and then commands simply "Fire!" if acting for an aimed duel. For a duel of command, as I have already shown, he says, "Are you ready?" Upon their affirmative response from the adversaries he commands "Fire! One, two, three!"

It would otherwise be better, as my advice, to not ask "Are you ready?" but instead say "Attention...Fire! One, two, three!" thus avoiding the adversaries having to reply with even a single word with weapons in hand.

(1) Sometimes one hands them over un-cocked, he must also command "Arm!" before the command to fire

As soon as the allowed time for an aimed duel has elapsed, or as soon as the last command has been pronounced, the director of combat and the witnesses seek to get between them, if necessary, to stop the adversaries and prevent them from firing. Then they see if they are wounded.

When the adversaries must exchange another ball, the director of combat replaces them and recommences the combat as before.

If there are any concerns about violations of the rules or conventions of combat, the director and the other witnesses are, as in the épée duel, required to decide whether to stop them or interrupt only the duel, after having made the appropriate observations.

The same rules equally apply as for the épée duel as to how to draw up the missive after the combat.

Printed in Great Britain
by Amazon